COWLEY PUBLICATIONS is a ministry of the brothers of the Society of Saint John the Evangelist, a monastic order in the Episcopal Church. Our mission is to provide books and resources for those seeking spiritual and theological formation. Cowley Publications is committed to developing a new generation of writers and teachers who will encourage people to think and pray in new ways about spirituality, reconciliation, and the future.

The Cost of Certainty

How religious conviction betrays
the human psyche

JEREMY YOUNG

COWLEY PUBLICATIONS
Cambridge, Massachusetts

To Anne,
who has taught me more than anyone else about love,
both human and divine.

Published in the United States of America by Cowley Publications,
a division of the Society of Saint John the Evangelist. No portion of this
book may be reproduced, stored in or introduced into a retrieval system,
or transmitted, in any form or by any means—including photocopying—
without the prior written permission of Cowley Publications, except in the
case of brief quotations embedded in critical articles and reviews.

Published by Darton, Longman and Todd, London, UK, 2004
Copyright © Jeremy Young

Library of Congress Cataloging-in-Publication Data:
Young, Jeremy, 1954–
   The cost of certainty : how religious conviction betrays the human psyche
/ Jeremy Young.
        p. cm.
   Includes bibliographical references and index.
   ISBN 1-56101-232-7 (pbk. : alk. paper)   1.   Christianity—Psychology.
2.   Polarity—Religious aspects—Christianity. 3.   Uncertainty—Religious
aspects—Christianity.   I. Title.
   BR110.Y68 2005
   230'.01'9—dc22

                                                              2005009450

The Scripture quotations in this publication are taken from the
New International Version © 1973, 1978, 1984 by International Bible Society.
Published by Hodder & Stoughton Limited.

Cover design: Gary Ragaglia

This book was printed in the United States of America on acid-free paper.

COWLEY PUBLICATIONS
4 Brattle Street
Cambridge, Massachusetts 02138
800-225-1534 • www.cowley.org

CONTENTS

ACKNOWLEDGEMENTS

This book has been over ten years in its genesis. It is, therefore, impossible adequately to acknowledge and thank all those who have influenced my thinking. It has developed from a minor dissertation for the degree of Master of Theology at Heythrop College, London, which was supervised by Fr Brendan Callaghan SJ, and whose title was 'The Persona of the Priest', edited sections of which have been incorporated into Chapters Two, Three and Four. However, the subject matter of this work has moved well beyond the focus of that dissertation to examine the psychological and social dynamics of Christian belief in general.

Amongst individuals who have either encouraged me along the way or read and commented on the manuscript I would particularly like to thank Jeffrey Heskins, Stephen Pattison, Deborah Wilde, Polly Young-Eisendrath, Demaris Wehr, Eric Hutchison, Lindsay Blyth, Denis Campbell, Jeanne Penman, Kerric Harvey, Jo McMahon, Tom and Dorothy West, Judith Chavasse, Jo Kennedy, Rebecca Gibson, Liam Roe and, finally, my wife, Anne, without whose unfailing patience, encouragement and acute critical insights this book would never have been completed.

CHAPTER ONE

The Gospels of Conditional and Unconditional Love

The Gospel of Conditional Love

Although the history of Christianity contains some very remarkable stories of heroic self-sacrifice and devotion to others, over the centuries the Christian Church and individual Christians have been guilty of innumerable evils committed in the name of Christ, ranging from persecutions, crusades and wars of religion to bigotry, sexual repression and hypocrisy. Apologists for Christianity usually claim that these are aberrations, that they are the consequence of the sinfulness of office holders or individual believers and do not in themselves point to any deficiency in traditional Christian teaching itself. This book will argue otherwise. It is my belief that many of the evil or injurious deeds performed by practising Christians originate in specific core Christian beliefs which are usually regarded as 'orthodox'. Far from being distortions of normal Christianity, such ills are engendered by it; and the more uncritically these beliefs are held, the more destructive they are likely to be.

The origin of the maleficent effects of Christianity is, I contend, to be found in the stark dualism enshrined in the belief in a Day of Judgement at which the human race will be separated into two groups: one which will be saved and go to eternal bliss in heaven, and the other which will be damned

1

and experience an eternity of torture. This division creates deep-seated anxiety in believers, who may fear for their eternal fate, and this anxiety, in turn, interacts with a fundamental ambiguity in mainstream Christian teaching about the love of God, namely, that although the Church claims that God's love is unconditional, he only accepts those humans into heaven who believe in Jesus Christ and have repented of their sins. The rest he damns. The 'unconditional' love of God is actually hedged about by conditions and the threat of damnation for those who do not fulfil them. The acceptance of Christians by their fellow believers is likewise often conditional upon their adherence to particular standards of action or belief. These conditions interact with the emotional needs of the devout in many destructive ways. Many Christians look for an emotional fulfilment in their faith that they do not find elsewhere, but the cost of achieving it may be to fit themselves into a straitjacket of behaviour and conviction that considerably limits or distorts their personalities, and which may even result in neurotic symptoms.

Furthermore, the central Christian symbol, the cross, is highly ambiguous and is open to a wide variety of interpretations. The traditional interpretation of Jesus' death as a sacrifice, expiation or atonement for sin, combined with the call, attributed to Christ, for each of us to take up our cross and follow him, has given rise to forms of spirituality and education that can be and frequently are psychologically damaging to believers. Very often the faithful have been encouraged to sacrifice themselves before they have developed sufficient of their own mature identity to have a self to sacrifice. In many different ways the cross has been used as a justification for the repression of genuine emotional growth and self-confidence in both children and adults.

Because of these presentations of its central doctrines, far from offering healing and liberation, the Christian faith may easily become an emotional, intellectual or spiritual prison, inhibiting the growth of churchgoers towards both psychological and spiritual maturity. The Christian gospel claims that

2

'the truth will set you free' (John 8:32), but so often the experience of living as a Christian in the Church is the exact opposite. Rather than being liberated from false restraints upon their lives, Christians frequently seem afraid of doing the 'wrong' thing or expressing the 'wrong' opinion. They may be excessively concerned about what others in their church or prayer group think about them, or express anxiety about whether or not God really loves them. They may even worry about whether or not they are damned. Fear and love are incompatible in Christian teaching, but fear, or at least anxiety, is one of the commonest of emotional states amongst the devout. It appears to be endemic to Christians. Such apprehension is not what the psalmist described as 'the fear of the Lord [which] is the beginning of wisdom' (Psalm 111:10), that is, the awe and reverence of God which is a necessary part of a healthy spiritual life, but is rather a product of emotional immaturity or inadequacy. The gospel is supposed to bring an experience of the love of God: 'perfect love drives out fear' (1 John 4:18), and of freedom: 'if the Son sets you free, you will be free indeed' (John 8:36), but the emotions of those within the confines of the Church are very frequently those of prisoners: fear; anger; blame; guilt; self-hatred; or, depression.

Conversely, some Christians are full of self-confidence, convinced that they have found the one and only truth that explains the mystery of the universe. They may claim that they possess a revelation from God and lay down very clear rules of behaviour that Christians are expected to follow, asserting that these are the Law of God. On the surface, such Christians seem to have very little in common with those who experience fear or anxiety, but there is an intimate connection between them: paradoxically, the source of assurance of the confident group is at the same time the source of worry for the anxious one; and the same person may at times be confident and at times fearful.

The reason for this paradox is the inconsistency (already referred to) between the two opposing presentations of God's love in the Bible and Christian doctrine: the one which says

3

that God loves us all unconditionally; the other which lays down necessary conditions of belief or behaviour before God will receive us. Traditional Christianity frequently reconciles the unconditional and conditional features of its conception of divine love by using a pattern of teaching found repeatedly in the Bible, and in the Church over the centuries, which states that God loves us all unconditionally and is, therefore, prepared to offer everybody, without exception, a relationship with him. However, at the same time, God's acceptance is presented as very much conditional on the response of the one who wishes to receive it, which means that *God's unconditional love only becomes operative as a relationship of acceptance and intimacy after the believer has fulfilled certain conditions.* These include a belief in his Son, Jesus Christ, as Lord and Saviour, incorporation into the Church through baptism (in many denominations) and a life lived according to Christian moral precepts. In this presentation, the fate of those who do not meet the conditions, however they are defined, is exclusion from God's presence, in other words, damnation. Although this teaching claims that God continues to love even the damned, his love does not benefit them; they remain in hell.

I call this interpretation of Christianity *the Gospel of Conditional Love* and believe that this is the understanding of the gospel which is responsible for the underlying anxiety experienced by so many practising Christians. The Gospel of Conditional Love causes untold problems for Christian spirituality and pastoral practice because, although it stresses the unconditional nature of God's love in theory, in practice it places much more emphasis upon its conditional nature. In essence, this version of the gospel states, at least implicitly, that, even if he loves us, God does not accept us as we are, but only insofar as we believe in Jesus and obey his commandments. This belief gives rise to *a contradiction at the heart of ecclesiastical practice: the Church says that God's love is unconditional and yet it constantly sets up conditions for acceptance within its fold.* The consequence is that those who do not fulfil

4

the conditions of inclusion are likely to find themselves subject to what they believe is God's condemnation and that of
their Christian communities as well.

This threat of condemnation or rejection gives rise to the
anxiety of fearful Christians, just as the assurance of salvation
is the source of the complacency of those who appear to have
no doubts. However, the latter's confidence often masks a
disguised doubt of their acceptability. Both groups, if they
allow themselves to be aware of the inclination of God (as
described by this teaching) to reject those who do not meet his
requirements and if they recognise their own failings or those
of their religious community, are likely to begin questioning
God's attitude towards themselves. Consequently, much
energy is expended by large numbers of believers in preventing themselves from acknowledging these possibilities, with
the result that a very great deal of church life is conditioned by
their manifold attempts to avoid seeing or engaging with
the uncomfortable negative sides of Christian belief and
behaviour.

Frequently Christians try to do this by attributing to their
convictions an unwarranted certainty. Certainty is hugely
appealing to the devout because it promises to take away their
anxiety through guaranteeing the truth of what they believe
and, hence, their acceptance by God. It provides the emotional
reassurance they require. However, any assertion of certainty,
whether by individuals or institutions, is a huge problem for
the contemporary Church because it is *a betrayal of genuine
Christian faith*. This may appear a strange thing to say when
the churches are losing so many of their members and when
those who remain inside them are confronted every day by so
much scepticism in wider society. Surely, Christians need to
have more confidence in their beliefs and the more certain
they become, the better? But this is to misunderstand the true
nature of faith.

Faith allows us to trust God and to feel confidence in what
we believe, but that confidence is very different from the
certainty that so many Christians seem to be seeking. Rather

than certainty, *faith may be described as an attitude of trust adopted in the face of our ignorance of God.* As the famous passage about faith in the Letter to the Hebrews says: 'Now faith is being sure of what *we hope for* and certain of *what we do not see'* (Hebrews 11:1, italics added). Paradoxically it is through trust in our *not knowing* that we come to knowledge of God. *As others have said, certainty is the opposite of faith. The quest for certain knowledge is one of the surest ways to destroy authentic Christian faith. Insofar as the Church colludes with or encourages the quest for certainty, it is betraying the foundations of the Christian understanding of and belief in God and, hence, the gospel itself.*

What I am saying is that a claim to possess certainty is an illegitimate attempt to deny human limitations and is also, in essence, *an attempt to live without faith.* Faith is a paradoxical possession. Although it may be adopted on 'reasonable grounds', faith always goes beyond the evidence because it takes the form of trust in an unseen God. Faith is precisely an attitude of trust which takes us further than unaided human reason or empirical observation can carry us. This is the case because God is not and, notwithstanding the incarnation, could never be an object in the phenomenal world; nor is God a scientific hypothesis which can be tested or demonstrated. Even though we may believe that we have observed the effects of his presence in our lives or in the phenomenal world, we cannot see God. For this reason, although it produces assurance in the believer, faith is not knowledge about something that can be demonstrated or proven. An attitude of faith may bring an internal experience of conviction of a sort, but it is not secured (however much it may be supported) by anything that can be known, experienced or observed in the normal manner of human apprehension of the external world.

When the nature and limitations of faith are forgotten Christianity easily becomes an irrational and dogmatic creed claiming absolute truth for itself and engaging in a power drive to suppress or destroy all alternative points of view and those who hold them. This is particularly the case when certainty is combined with the Gospel of Conditional Love, when Christians who believe in the Gospel of Conditional Love and who, consequently, are subject to the anxiety of rejection in their relationship with God, resort to an assertion of certainty as a means of protecting themselves from that anxiety. In itself, the Gospel of Conditional Love is hugely influential upon the internal dynamics of the Christian churches; all the more so because it is so often associated with the desire for certainty. Its effects may be quite subtle and not obviously connected with their emotional source or they may be very serious indeed. They include:

- the desire for certainty itself, often combined with a resistance to thinking about difficult questions or engaging with contemporary culture;
- the restriction of the lives of Christians by narrow, legalistic or puritanical rules of behaviour;
- the development of neurotic illnesses in practising Christians;
- the use of Christianity, or a particular denominational allegiance, as a mark of community membership and as a reason to exclude, denigrate or persecute those who are different;
- the occurrence of controlling or power-driven behaviour by 'servants of the Church';
- the covering up of misbehaviour by members of the clergy, including the sexual abuse of children, in order to protect the Church from scandal;
- the scapegoating or persecution of those who have different beliefs or ethical standards;
- and, ultimately, war and genocide.

Although these outcomes may appear very wide-ranging and unconnected with each other, this book will identify the links between them and the complicated and often hidden patterns of interaction that are sustained by the Gospel of Conditional Love and its bedfellow, the quest for certainty.

My Early Experience of the Gospel of Conditional Love

My own induction into the Gospel of Conditional Love happened at the age of sixteen during a school trip to see the Oberammergau Passion Play. The play made the Christian faith seem real to me for the first time, and so 'I gave my life to Jesus as my Lord and Saviour' at 8.25 a.m. on 23 August 1970. Immediately I experienced an overwhelming sense of the presence of Christ and was convinced that I had found the meaning of life. When I returned home I made my family's life miserable by trying to convert them. Unaccountably, they did not immediately see the light and become Christians. Life gradually settled into a new pattern. I joined a local conservative Evangelical church, started studying Religious Knowledge for 'A' level (Leaving Certificate) and became very involved in the Christian Discussion Circle at school, the equivalent of a Christian Union. I also became intolerant and puritan.

The teaching which I received at my church, and at the Christian house parties that I attended, stressed God's love for us. However, we were also told that God is holy and just and that, apart from Jesus, he could have nothing to do with us, because of our sinfulness. Holiness and sin cannot mix. Often this point was illustrated using the big black floppy leather Bible the speakers seemed always to possess, and which they used to indicate the nature of sin. The Bible was placed on one of their hands, which represented ourselves, to show the weight of sin separating us from God, who was imagined as being above us. Then it would be flipped onto the other hand, representing Jesus, to show that he received the whole of our sin and suffered the separation that should have been ours. The hand representing us, now freed from sin, was lifted up to indicate that the way back to God was clear. Jesus' death as a sacrifice for sin on our behalf was said to demonstrate God's great love for us, so great that he did not hesitate to send his only Son to die for us.

The speakers did not explain how it was that Jesus subsequently returned to his Father despite being separated from him by our sins, nor did they seem to be aware either of the irony of using the Bible to represent sin or of the equivocal emotional effect that could be generated from this depiction of God. When one reflects upon this account of the gospel, it becomes clear that the nature of God's love contained within it is severely limited. Only by ignoring or rationalising away the negative side of this teaching is it possible for a Christian to enter into a relationship of secure trust with God. In other words, Christians who believe this account of the gospel message have to find some way of minimising or excluding from their awareness the punitive and terrifying aspect of God's character, namely, that he will condemn to eternal torment in hell those who do not accept Christ as their Saviour.

There are many accounts of the nature of hell that attempt to justify God's behaviour theologically, largely by suggesting that such punishment is in some way an expression of his justice or else that, rather than God rejecting the damned, it is they who refuse to enter into a loving relationship with him. But even if such explanations have some force, the punitive images of God contained in the Bible, and repeatedly used throughout the Christian centuries in preaching and instruction, have had and continue to have damaging emotional effects. Since stories of God's wrath and condemnation have been continuously read in the liturgy of the Church, which claims to teach that God is love, it is hardly surprising that the message of God's tendency to punish has often had more impact upon believers than that of his forgiveness of sinners. The result is unavoidably that churchgoers' belief in God's love is very likely to be undermined by a fear of his wrath. And this fear has been powerfully reinforced by the frequent use of this teaching about hell by those in positions of ecclesiastical or political authority as a means to frighten people into social conformity. Many Christians must have refrained from such 'sins' as disobedience of their superiors or political agitation, amongst many others, because they feared eternal consequences.

Looking back now, it seems clear to me that the emotional message I actually received from my initial acceptance of Christian teaching was definitely not that God loved me unconditionally. Rather, it was that his love for me could easily turn to rejection. In some part of myself I believed that God would only continue to love me if I continued to be good enough and to believe the right things about him. Such an emotional conviction about God is not going to encourage deep trust or confidence. Instead, *those who feel like this will be very careful not to upset this God, and will definitely not believe that they are accepted as the people they happen to be. As a consequence, they will try very hard to become what they are supposed to be, and may pretend to be better than they are.* That, at least, was my experience and, I know, that of many of my fellow young Christians.

Although we believed that we were loved by God, and that we were accepted by him on the basis of Jesus' sacrifice and not for any merit of our own, we continued to be influenced by an all-pervasive anxiety about sinning. The paradox was that, although Jesus had supposedly set us free from sin, we all continued to be sinners. Since we were forgiven, this continuing sinfulness should not have been a cause of worry. We should have been content to do our best and then to relax and trust God. If sanctification is the work of the Holy Spirit, why should we have been anxious about it? But we were. Part of the reason was, I believe, that the churches we belonged to, whilst preaching a Gospel of Unconditional Love, actually practised a Gospel of Conditional Love. We were afraid of rejection by our co-religionists, let alone by God, and this fear was strongly supported by the biblical depiction of God.

The Conditional Nature of God's Love in the Bible

Many passages in the Bible as a whole, and also some of the teaching it attributes to Jesus specifically, present repentance as a precondition of God's acceptance and threaten God's rejection for those who do not repent, and this applies just as much to those who are already within the Jewish or Christian communities as to those who are outside. Later on it will be necessary to discuss how we may interpret the Bible as a witness to the unconditional love of God in the light of this fact (see Chapter Six). For the moment, I will simply give a brief indication of the ways in which the Bible presents God's love as conditional and sketch some of the consequences, both historical and contemporary, for traditional Christian spirituality and the life of the churches.

The distinction in Christian doctrine between those accepted and those rejected by God grows out of an inheritance from earlier Jewish thinking: the division between the people chosen by God and those who are not chosen. Although there are undeniably universalistic elements in the Jewish faith, for example, the Jews will bring other nations to know God (Isaiah 42:6–7), there are also very strong traditions emphasising the special and exclusive relationship between God and the Jews, and the need for the Jews to remain separate from other nations in order to protect that relationship (e.g. Nehemiah 13:23–30). The Jews are portrayed as having a special role and destiny in the purposes of God and a special relationship with him. In theological terms, this is referred to as a *covenant*. This means that there is an agreement between God and the Jews, one which was made first with Abraham (Genesis 17) and later renewed with Moses, during a ceremony in which young bulls were sacrificed and the people were sprinkled with 'the blood of the covenant' (Exodus 24). According to the terms of this agreement, God undertakes to be the God of the Jews and to give them the land of Canaan and, in return, they undertake to circumcise their male children and to obey his Law, including the observation of the Sabbath. The benefits of this agreement for the Jews, the people whom God rescued out of slavery in Egypt, include the gift of the Promised Land, but the disadvantage is that they will be punished if they break God's commandments. The Hebrew Bible is in large part an account of how this covenant relationship developed, including the disobedience and unfaithfulness of the Jews and the punishments and forgiveness of God.

The Christian Church claims to be the New Israel and to inherit the promises of God to Israel, explicitly putting Christians in the same relationship of exclusivity and preference with God as the Jews. In other words, Christians believe that God's favour rests on them in the same way as it used to rest on the Jews and in a manner in which it does not rest on other peoples. This assertion is reinforced by the application of the covenant relationship to the Church. In Christian theology Christ is said to have inaugurated a new covenant between God and the Church (Hebrews 8) and his blood is regarded as 'the blood of the eternal covenant' (Hebrews 13:20). This is the doctrinal justification for the use by Christians of terms such as 'the People of God' to refer to Christian believers as a whole or, more restrictively, to those who belong to a particular denomination – as if the rest of humanity were not also people of God.

The use by Christianity of this covenant theology derived from Judaism is, it seems to me, the origin of a major problem for Christian doctrine, namely, the tension between: (a) the inclusive claim that God is the God of all peoples and willing to welcome everyone into a relationship with him, and (b) the exclusive claim that only those who repent and become Christians, accepting Christ's death as a sacrifice for their sins, will be saved.

Judaism originated as the religion of a group of nomadic tribes and developed into that of a particular settled people in the land between the River Jordan and the Mediterranean Sea. As such, the fact that the God of the Jews showed a remarkable preference for this particular people did not create a theological problem. Indeed, scholars suggest that it was only gradually that the Jews developed a conception of their 'god' as also the 'God' of all the world and all peoples. However, for Christianity, which from its conception has been a universal religion, the partiality of God for one section of the human population over all the rest creates a problem. The tension between universalistic and exclusivist tendencies in traditional Christianity underlies the tension between the unconditional and conditional understandings of God's love found in Christian teaching. The problems which I am examining in this book arise because much Christian teaching is ambiguous about whether it is truly a religion of God's grace towards all people or merely the religion of that exclusive minority who fulfil the conditions for receiving God's favour.

A major contributory factor to the anxiety of believers is the often punitive, at times seemingly arbitrary, behaviour of God. This arises because being in a covenant relationship with God does not by any means guarantee his favour and protection. Although, on the one hand, God's love for the Jewish people is an act of pure grace, completely unearned and dependent upon none of their own virtues or qualities, on the other hand, his favour towards them is frequently presented by the Bible as conditional upon their continuing good behaviour. Such is the negative aspect of the covenant relationship. As Moses tells them:

> For you are a people holy to the LORD your God. The LORD your God has chosen you out of all the peoples on the face of the earth to be his people, his treasured possession. The LORD did not set his affection on you and choose you because you were more numerous than other peoples, for you were the fewest of all peoples. But it was because the LORD loved you and kept the oath he swore to your forefathers, that he brought you out with a mighty hand and redeemed you from the land of slavery, from the power of Pharaoh king of Egypt. Know therefore that the LORD your God is God; he is the faithful God, keeping his covenant of love to a thousand generations of those who love him and keep his commands. But those who hate him he will repay to their face by destruction; he will not be slow to repay to their face those who hate him. Therefore, take care to follow the commands, decrees and laws I give you today. (Deuteronomy 7:6–11)

In confirmation of this view of God, the Hebrew Scriptures contain numerous examples of a wrathful God punishing his chosen people, other nations and specific individuals for their transgressions.

Contrary to the popular idea that the God of the New Testament is loving and forgiving as opposed to the angry God of the Old Testament, New Testament teaching frequently follows the same covenant pattern as the Old: God's love is given unconditionally; it cannot be earned, but in return he expects a response of good behaviour and right belief and he punishes those who do not give it. Even when the *unconditional* love of God is stressed by the New Testament, it is often associated with *conditions*. Consider, for example, these words in St John's Gospel: 'For God so loved the world that he gave his one and only Son, that whoever believes in him shall not perish but have eternal life. For God did not send his Son into the world to condemn the world, but to save the world through him' (John 3:16–17). These words, attributed to Jesus, are frequently used in evangelism to convey the unconditional love of God. He was prepared to send his Son to die for us when we were still sinners. How wonderful his love must be! However, the rest of the passage is quoted much less often: 'Whoever believes in him is not condemned, but whoever does not believe stands condemned already because he has not believed in the name of God's one and only Son' (John 3:18). St John appears to be saying that acceptance by God is conditional upon belief in his Son. Those who do not accept his Son are already condemned. Consider also these words in St Matthew's Gospel, also attributed to Jesus:

> 'Then he [the King] will say to those on his left, "Depart from me, you who are cursed, into the eternal fire prepared for the devil and his angels. For I was hungry and you gave me nothing to eat, I was thirsty and you gave me nothing to drink, I was a stranger and you did not invite me in, I needed clothes and you did not clothe me, I was sick and in prison and you did not look after

me . . ." Then they will go away to eternal punishment, but the righteous to eternal life.' (Matthew 25:41–3, 46)

This passage makes eternal life conditional upon charitable behaviour and threatens eternal punishment to those who do not practise it.

Examples of the presentation of God's love in the Bible as conditional could be multiplied at great length, but it is not my intention to do this. Nor am I concerned to arrive at an academic assessment of the history of these passages and the contexts of their writing and interpretation. Whilst such concerns are important, they are beside the point in the present task. What concerns me here is how such images of God, and accounts of his behaviour, have influenced the ways in which Christians have come to conceive of God and to respond to him. In other words, how these stories and their associated teachings, as they have been heard by ordinary Christians without benefit of scholarship and in the context of parish worship and instruction, have interacted with their emotional and psychological development to create their personal images of God and patterns of religious life; and also how the Church has used these passages to inculcate obedience and docility in its members. For centuries it has exposed Christians to the prospect of punishment, the Day of Judgement, often depicted in gruesome detail in murals on church walls, at which the eternal fate of humankind will be decided: some people going to bliss in heaven and others to torture in hell. All those pictures of the Day of Judgement in medieval churches and cathedrals, and the preaching of the terrors of hell throughout the Christian centuries, must powerfully have reinforced both their sense that God's love is only for those of whom he approves, and also the anxiety of those who were concerned about their eternal fate.

Jesus and the Gospel of Unconditional Love

In contrast to the Gospel of Conditional Love, there is a very great deal in the Bible as a whole, and especially in the New Testament, which suggests that God's love is unconditional and is intended for all people: for example, the Parable of the Prodigal Son in which the father runs to meet the disgraced son and kills the fatted calf out of his joy that his spendthrift son has returned (Luke 15:11–32), and the Parable of the Lost Sheep in which the shepherd leaves the ninety-nine and goes in search of the one who is missing (Luke 15:1–7). The unconditional and gracious core of the gospel is particularly apparent in Jesus' attitude to the social and religious outcasts of his time. There are several examples of Jesus treating acknowledged 'sinners' with particular compassion, including the woman caught in adultery (John 8:1–11), the woman who anointed Jesus (Luke 7:36–50) and Zacchaeus, the tax collector (Luke 19:1–10). The most important implication of Jesus' behaviour is that God loves us unconditionally and accepts us *prior to any response* that we may make to his love. Jesus' initiative somehow frees people to respond. *The response is not the condition of acceptance, but the means by which the discovery of already being accepted is manifested in their lives.*

In my opinion, the distinction between God's acceptance *following from and being conditional upon* repentance or conversion, and acceptance *being the basis upon which it becomes possible* for repentance or conversion to occur, is absolutely vital to the development of a form of the Christian religion that is free from the polarising and exclusionary attitudes that feature so prominently in traditional Christianity. Only if God's grace genuinely encompasses the whole of a person, good and bad, can true healing and the concomitant transformation of the individual personality become possible.

As St Paul repeatedly stressed, there is no possibility of earning our way into God's favour. Sister Martha Reeves describes the implications of this insight well:

> Theological and political debate may rage, yet for Christians there is but one example of caring: that of Jesus, who spent most of his life being ritually unclean because

> he associated with those people whom 'respectable' society had cast out. It was by humbly entering into relationship, through the relationship itself, that Jesus' forgiveness was offered and received. Jesus did not demand that people made public acts of repentance in order to have forgiveness. He reached through all barriers to the person, and it was in the freedom of this truly loving relationship that redemptive life could begin to flower. (Reeves, 1987, p. 14)

This was good news for those whom the Jewish Law designated as sinful and those who were social outcasts, but not for any who regarded themselves as righteous.

The implication of Jesus' behaviour is that followers of Jesus do not have to fulfil the requirements of the Law and become sinless before they are accepted by him, and even their continuing sinfulness after they have responded to the good news does *not* exclude them from relationship with God. Rather, their sin may become a continuing motivation to return to God. The theologian Kevin Kelly describes sin as a positive word because 'the very "owning" of one's sinfulness (and sin) before God is a transformative act. It is the first step on the road to conversion' (Kelly, 1993, p. 107). Kelly adds:

> 'Sinner' used in this positive way should not be taken to mean 'someone who used to be a sinner but is so no longer'. That is not what the tax-collector (in the parable) means when he prays, 'Lord, be merciful to me, a sinner'. He really is a sinner and he recognises himself as such. That is precisely why he recognises his need for the compassion and forgiveness of God. Even the words of Jesus to the woman taken in adultery, 'Go, and sin no more', are not an indication that she is no longer a sinner. She leaves Jesus a sinner, but a forgiven sinner, as do many others who hear his life-giving words 'Go, your sins are forgiven you.' (Kelly, 1993, pp. 107–8)

In contrast, Kelly points out, there are those for whom sin

has a negative meaning; these are the self-righteous as represented by the Pharisee in the parable. 'It is as though the only sin that ties the hand of God's forgiveness is the sin of grounding one's self-worth on a belief in the non-worth of everyone else' (Kelly, 1993, p. 108). This is the attitude at the heart of Pharisaism: 'I thank thee, O God, that I am not like the rest of men, greedy, dishonest, adulterous; or, for that matter, like this tax-gatherer' (Luke 18:11) (Kelly, 1993, p. 118).

Jesus and the Pharisees

The spirituality of the Pharisees is presented in the Gospels as the opposite of the good news which Jesus proclaimed. Nevertheless, *Pharisaism* is not dead, but is very much alive and thriving in the contemporary Church. In essence, Pharisaism is another name for the Gospel of Conditional Love and involves the following claims:

• we know what God's commandments are;
• we can fulfil them;
• God's acceptance of us is conditional upon fulfilling those injunctions;
• others are inferior to us and rejected by God because they do not meet his requirements.

The Pharisee, who believes that he is living according to God's Law, separates himself from those who are not in order to preserve himself from moral or ritual contagion. He also, like his colleague in the parable, boosts his own sense of self-worth by comparing himself favourably with those who do not keep the Law.

Jesus was persecuted by the Pharisees because he challenged their elitist and separatist use of the Jewish religion. He included within the grace of God those who did not live up to the strict standards of the Law. The Pharisees in the Gospels represent the way in which a genuine faith in God and desire to do his will can be subtly perverted into a form of unconscious opposition to him. They oppose the Son of

God in the name of God and eventually murder him. *A central contention of this book is that this process is lived out again and again today in the lives of the devout and in the institutional practices of the churches, and that a central feature of Christian Pharisaism is a belief, however well disguised, that God's love is ultimately conditional.*

However, the term 'Pharisaism' should be used with caution. The Pharisees were influential rabbis, of whom St Paul was originally one, who sought to interpret the Law of God strictly and to ensure that it was followed in minute detail. Because of the conflict between the early Christians and the Jewish establishment, they have had a very bad press in the New Testament and in subsequent Christian teaching and preaching. Consequently, the standard Christian interpretation of their behaviour and attitudes is one-sided and, very likely, a distortion. Certainly, many Jewish and Christian scholars would claim so. Here, I use 'Pharisaism' not to refer to what the historical Pharisees were actually like, but to the depiction of them in Christian invective. In many respects they were highly virtuous; many became the saints of later rabbinic Judaism. Indeed, Jesus is recorded as saying: 'I tell you that unless your righteousness surpasses that of the Pharisees and the teachers of the law, you will certainly not enter the kingdom of God' (Matthew 5:20).

Here, I am concerned not with the behaviour of individual historical Pharisees, but with the attitudes represented by the biblical Pharisees within the Christian tradition, in particular, their conception of the Law of God. They were opposed to those teachings and actions of Jesus which expressed unconditional love towards sinners. Pharisaism cannot tolerate the freedom of God to accept anyone God chooses even if she or he does not fulfil the conditions laid down in the Law. Such divine freedom breaks the rules by which the Pharisee seeks to guarantee his own acceptance by God and his distinctiveness from those who do not obey them. It destroys the grounds of his self-assertion and religious assurance, because it destroys the conditions through which the Pharisee seeks to establish his superiority and, very often, to control other people as well. This accounts for the anger of the Jewish leaders (as depicted in the Gospels) at the behaviour of Jesus, who not only broke the Law himself, but also consorted with notorious sinners.

Jesus' behaviour undermined the whole Pharisaical approach to God by taking away the conditions that were its lifeblood. He directly challenged their interpretation of the Law of God and, in addition, accused them of hypocrisy and standing in the way of those who wished to respond to God (Matthew 23; Luke 11:37–52). This was good news, but not for those who could not give up conditionality. For them it was lawlessness and blasphemy, to be met with the proper response under the Law: the capital punishment of the one who was lawless and blasphemous. In other words, they had to destroy Jesus, who threatened their religious system, in order to protect that system and to prevent themselves from becoming conscious of how far they were themselves in rebellion against God. They excluded and scapegoated the 'sinner' Jesus from the community to preserve its 'purity' and their own conviction that they were loyal to and accepted by God. This is precisely what those who propagate the Gospel of Conditional Love continue to do in the contemporary Church: they murder Christ anew but in the name of the gospel, which they have turned into a new version of the Law, and tragically they do so in the conviction that this is the will of God and out of a real, but misguided, desire to serve him.

In contrast to the biblical Pharisees and the modern proponents of the Gospel of Conditional Love, those who genuinely acknowledge themselves as sinners have the opportunity to recognise Jesus as the one who comes offering a transformed relationship with God. Even so, the meeting with him is likely to be uncomfortable because it always contains elements of both mercy and judgement: mercy because Jesus offers us new life as friends of God which can be entered into without preconditions; judgement because he contradicts our current way of life and challenges us to change. The biblical Pharisees aborted the possibility of allowing Jesus into their lives by refusing to accept his judgement. As far as they were concerned, they were in all essentials already living under the rule of God. Their mistake was not to realise that they were still subject to sin at the core of their being and that they were guilty of profound rebellion against God, ironically disguised as obedience to his Law. Instead, they identified themselves and their behaviour with a virtue that did not yet exist. Indeed, their adherence to the overt commands of God was one of the chief ways in which sin ruled their lives: it blinded them to the reality of their condition and prevented them from repenting. In this way *their religion became a form of opposition to God.* This is also what tends to happen nowadays to those who practise the Gospel of Conditional Love in the Church; their Christian faith takes the form of Pharisaism and they become proponents of a religion of Law which is implicitly opposed to the Gospel of Unconditional Love and the essential message of Jesus Christ. This is a great tragedy because, as a result of this perversion of the gospel, the lives of many Christians are seriously stunted, and the ability of the Church as a whole to communicate the genuine gospel of God's unconditional love is seriously inhibited.

The Human Fear of God's Love

A very important reason, I suggest, why the Gospel of Conditional Love and the Pharisaical attitudes associated with it, are so common amongst contemporary Christians is that most of us, despite our protestations of faith, actually fear God's love. We need to understand why this is so if we are to change the current state of affairs. There is a paradox in human nature: although we long for a deep and intimate relationship with God and the full acceptance of ourselves as we are, we are unable, for the most part, to tolerate such acceptance if it should come our way. Such an inability is frequently hidden in the secret places of the Pharisee's soul and that of anyone, whether Christian or not, who runs away from true intimacy with God.

Significantly, this resistance to emotional closeness is not just a feature of human relationships with God; it is found very commonly in relationships between people. It is disturbing how often those who come for psychotherapy complain about their isolation and loneliness whilst at the same time pushing away or ignoring others who might offer them friendship or love, as though truly getting close to another person represents some kind of threat to their sense of identity, even to their existence itself. How much more so with God! Many people live out their lives in either physical or emotional isolation because they cannot risk allowing anyone else to be genuinely intimate with them. They may have been subjected to abusive or neglectful forms of upbringing, or it may be that they have such a low opinion of themselves that they do not believe that anyone would want to be with them if they knew what they were really like. Alternatively or in addition, they may be unable to accept certain aspects of themselves and unconsciously realise that if they were to permit someone else really to know them, they themselves would have to acknowledge their full personalities, including their sin, weakness and mistakes, or even their strengths and virtues. Since this would be too humiliating or distressing or challenging for them, they dare not risk the exposure and self-knowledge that such a relationship would involve.

In an analogous manner, accepting the idea of a God who loves us as we are may be experienced, consciously or unconsciously, as a threat by Christians. Such a being might show total acceptance and understanding of those parts of ourselves that we have rejected and might even encourage us to learn to love them ourselves. (Indeed, this is the implicit requirement of Christ's commandment to love our neighbours *as ourselves*.) *To be truly loved is an invitation to develop an integrity and an honesty about ourselves of which few of us are presently capable, and which most of us fear.* Because of this fear, many people, I believe, including those who claim to be religiously commit-

22

ted, tend to withdraw from too much genuine engagement with God, and this tendency is reinforced by the fact that God is not simply someone who affirms us as we are; he also challenges us to realise our potential for growth into our redeemed humanity. In other words, *his love is not an easy love to receive because he not only invites us to know and love ourselves, but also challenges us to change into the people we would become if we were completely open to his presence at the centre of our lives.*

Regrettably, God's challenge to change may be misinterpreted by those individuals who find it difficult to love themselves, because such people normally find it impossible to believe that anyone else could truly love them, including God. Ironically, whilst longing for such acceptance, they may push away the one who really does love them as they are. Even so, the Christian belief that God wants them to change for the better may give them the impression that if they try hard enough they may be able to earn his approval. Consequently, they may continue to seek his love, but do so through attempting, consciously or unconsciously, to deserve it. In this case, they will attempt to be 'good enough for God' and be constantly fearful that, if they fail, God will reject them. This is a major reason why such people are so often anxious.

All of us live in ways which are limited by the selfish and hurtful actions of which we are guilty or by the compromises we have made over the years. It may be that we have sacrificed some element of our integrity. It may be that our lack of confidence or our fear has inhibited us from undertaking certain projects or entering particular relationships. It may be that we have put ourselves at the centre of our lives and ignored the needs of others. It may be that we have deliberately harmed others or lived without regard to the consequences of our actions upon others. If so, we have injured our humanity and meeting with God will make us aware of this and invite us to live more authentically. Some of us are able to respond positively to this invitation, but others react defensively instead. There can be a certain security in a restrictive and law-bound form of religion which an engagement with the disruptive and liberating Spirit of God inevitably threatens. Freedom can be even more frightening than love because it gives us the possibility of change and takes away the safe confinement of our previous pattern of living. True spiritual freedom opens up the unlimited possibility of continual growth and development through our relationship with God; it also strips us of the defences we have used against him, including legalistic religion. This is why Jesus' preaching and behaviour were so intolerable to the Pharisees and why their present-day successors continue to convert the gospel into the Law at every opportunity.

There is a paradox in the love of God: he accepts us unconditionally as we are and yet he invites us to be transformed through our relationship with him. In theological language, he comes to 'save us from sin'; in other words, he takes the initiative to rescue us from all that distorts, restricts or destroys the fullness of our humanity. The essence of sin is to make yourself your own God. To sin is to put yourself or something other than God at the centre of your life, to give primary value to anything other than God. Christian spirituality is fundamentally about the restoration of the relationship of individual believers and social groups to God and to each other. In Christian thinking the consequence of replacing God, who is truly the origin and centre of each person's life, with something else is to introduce disorder into a human personality, and this disorder is expressed in those actions which are destructive of self and others. The same applies at a corporate level: when the truly loving God is displaced from being at the centre of the common life of a community, an imbalance in relationships results which is expressed in various forms of sin, such as narrow-mindedness, injustice, violence, oppression and exploitation – all too often justified by appeal to a 'God' we ourselves have created in the image of our own violence.

The tension between the views that God accepts us unconditionally and that he wants us to change has, I suggest, given rise to the confusion between conditional and unconditional love in Christian teaching. What has happened is that *God's desire for us to change has been interpreted as a rejection of the people we are before we change.* Because the activity of God includes guiding us towards the eradication of sinfulness, God can very easily be misunderstood to be asking us to give up sin before he will accept us. In a sense, this is true: if our sinfulness is understood as a rejection of relationship with God, giving up sin is the same as opening oneself to a genuine meeting with God. However, a problem arises when sin is understood, not as a general condition of alienation from God in which we worship ourselves, but as *sins*, the particular actions that give evidence that we are not living with integrity, and that God is not at the centre of our lives, such as greed, lust, pride, sloth and aggression. Such a conception of sin as sins cannot achieve psychological integration because, according to this way of thinking, whatever is regarded as sinful must forever be rejected and fought against or else we will not be accepted by God. Christian spirituality from this perspective becomes a constant struggle to grow in 'holiness' through our own efforts; in other words, to live without doing those actions or thinking those thoughts that are considered to be sinful. This is the spirituality of the Pharisees. An alternative spiritual way is based on the recognition that sin is only overcome when the *whole* personality is enabled by God's grace to turn towards him. If any part of an individual is excluded from that relationship, it remains antagonistic towards God, and that person's reconciliation with God is only partial.

The spirituality of Pharisaism is based on a misunderstanding of sin. Sin is not the same as sins: it is a fundamental orientation of the personality towards the wishes and apprehensions of the ego (the conscious self) and away from God. Sin cannot be overcome by efforts of will aimed at resisting temptation, the desire to commit particular unacceptable actions. Paradoxically, it is quite possible for people to live more moral lives using their wills in this way but, in doing so, to grow no closer to God; they may even move farther away. Indeed, one who succeeds in resisting temptation may fall into the sin of spiritual pride (traditionally regarded as the most deadly of sins) about that achievement. This is one reason why Pharisaism cannot work.

Sin is only overcome by the discovery that God is truly the centre and source of all our life and that relating to God is a source of joy and freedom. As a result of this discovery in an individual's life, it becomes possible for that person to change. Even so, a meeting with God is likely to awaken a sense of failure, guilt, shame, humiliation and wickedness. This is because when we begin to become aware of God, we also become aware of our manifold resistance to God (that is, 'our sin') for we want to keep control of our own lives; but, whereas before this encounter being in charge of ourselves through asserting the independence and self-direction of our ego seemed good and desirable, it now starts to appear rather shabby and selfish. Thus, there is an ambiguity about encountering God: on the one hand, we become aware of his love and acceptance of us as we are and, on the other hand, we begin to be aware in new and unexpected ways of our own grubbiness and sin; and the latter awareness may seem like God's judgement or condemnation of ourselves as evildoers.

However, a point which Christians often overlook, and which I believe is vital to an eradication of the Gospel of Conditional Love, is that *God's judgement and forgiveness are deeply interwoven and always occur at the same time – we are the ones who separate them, not God – and, furthermore, that our repentance is dependent upon our reception of God's forgiveness, not the other way around.* These ideas may seem strange to many who have received traditional Christian religious instruction, so I would ask anyone who is unfamiliar with them to take seriously the possibility that an authentic encounter with God brings both judgement (God shows us who we are and what we need to change) and forgiveness (God shows us that we are loved and accepted whatever we may have done); and that these are accompanied by his grace (his initiative to free us from whatever binds or limits our response to him) enabling us to repent (to realise we need to begin living differently and to give our consent to change). This is the under-standing of our relationship with God which I am advocating in this book. The emotional reality is that *only if God's love, for-giveness and acceptance are regarded as the foundation and pre-condition for our ability to repent and change, rather than as the consequence of our repentance, will the Christian religion be able to function as a truly liberating and transformative system of belief. If not, it will inevitably create restrictive forms of religious practice and bind believers in the chains of anxiety and fear.*

CHAPTER TWO

The Closing of the Christian Mind

The Boundary Conditions of the Church

Christian belief and membership of the Church are some of the most important means by which individuals seek for an emotional security and satisfaction that they may not find elsewhere in their lives. One of the ways they do this is to look for a sense of belonging and acceptance through their church membership. However, there is a problem: whenever individuals join a church they are inducted into a society of Christians who, in most cases and within varying limits, expect them to behave in certain ways and to express certain beliefs. In order to belong to a Christian congregation it is usually necessary to conform to such local norms to a significant extent. All social groups have expectations of the behaviour and beliefs of their members and limits to the degree of diversity that they will tolerate. Too much non-conformity may result in sanctions of one sort or another, ranging from the expression of disapproval through social ostracism to imprisonment and, ultimately, exile or the death penalty. Acceptance of individuals by a group entails the acceptance by those individuals of some form of restriction upon their self-expression. Whether these conditions of membership are broad or narrow, willingly agreed by members or experienced by them as an imposition, they will always exist.

Even if God's acceptance is completely unconditional, the Church as an institution within human society cannot avoid drawing some boundaries around itself and saying that some people belong and others do not. Even the most inclusive adherents of the Christian religion cannot claim that all human beings belong to the visible human institutions which carry the name of 'Church'. Many belong to other religions or repudiate religious affiliation of any kind. To give an obvious example, a Christian is expected to believe in Jesus Christ and not Allah. Most Christians and Moslems would have extreme difficulties in accepting as legitimate co-religionists others who worship both Christ and Allah. On the face of it, Christian and Moslem beliefs are incompatible and it is not possible to belong to both religious communities at the same time.

In contrast, there is a considerable ambiguity about the boundaries between Christian belief and Zen Buddhist practice. Zen meditation practice does not involve any explicit acknowledgement of a god, and a number of Christian priests and members of religious communities practise Zen. Some have even been authorised as official teachers of Zen with the title *roshi*, whilst continuing to act as Christian priests and religious. Even so, many conservative Christians would find such a mixture of Zen and Christianity unacceptable, and some would exclude anyone pursuing both traditions from membership of their congregations.

All institutions have boundaries: those people within them belong; those outside do not. The Church has to have some criteria of membership if it is to stand for anything at all. It has always been the case that there have been minimum standards of belief and behaviour to which Christians have been required to conform by the Church. These have varied in strictness over the centuries but they have always existed. Any criterion is bound to exclude some people and thus *suggest that they are not acceptable to God*. Consequently, there have always been those who have found themselves at the edge of the Church or outside it because of their scepticism or heresy or morally unacceptable behaviour. *When admission to the Church is made conditional upon fulfilling certain expectations of belief or behaviour, some people are told, explicitly or implicitly, that they are not good enough for God.*

An everyday practice that illustrates how such conditions of membership function in the local church is the baptism of infants. This is a particularly controversial issue in the Church of England because the Church exists in a society which used to be almost exclusively Christian, but which has become pluralist and secular. The issue of the identity and definition of its membership is particularly troublesome because its membership used to be almost coterminous with the English population, and was supported by strong legal sanctions against those minorities who did not belong. This identification of Anglicanism with Englishness has gradually been eroded until regular attenders at worship in the Church of England now represent a very small minority of the total population. Committed Anglicans are a tiny remnant in English society amongst a host of atheists, agnostics, Roman Catholics, Non-Conformists, and members of other religions. The contemporary reality of pluralism puts in question the Church of England's claim to be the church of the nation. When even the vast majority of those who have a nominal Anglican identity hardly ever come to church, it is not surprising that many clergy feel that the lines of demarcation should be drawn more distinctly.

In view of this situation, a number of the clergy will accept the children of practising churchgoers for baptism, because they will be brought up as Christians, but will not agree to baptise the children of the lapsed or uncommitted. They have strong arguments to support their views. Chief amongst these is the fact that in the baptism service the parents of the child to be baptised have to promise to bring their child up as a Christian. Parents also have to make certain professions of Christian faith and commitment for themselves and for their child. Not unreasonably, those clergy who oppose indiscriminate baptism point out that parents who are not practising Christians cannot make these promises in good faith. On these grounds they withhold baptism from those who do not satisfy them that they are committed Christians. Alternatively, they insist that parents attend church regularly for several weeks and take part in a course of instruction before they will permit their child to be baptised. They may offer a Service of Thanksgiving for the Birth of a Child as an alternative to those who are not yet able to make a Christian commitment and attend church regularly. Some will also refuse baptism to a second child if parents have not fulfilled their promises concerning a Christian upbringing for their first child. Paradoxically, those who operate such strict baptism policies often claim that they do not refuse baptism to any child, but leave it up to the parents to make the decision for themselves once they have understood the implications.

The unfortunate result of such policies is that *thousands of parents believe themselves to be unwelcome in the Church of England.* Frequently they are convinced that they were refused baptism or were fobbed off with a Service of Thanksgiving, which was not what they wanted. I have often met such parents, especially when I worked as a part-time hospital chaplain. The anger and resentment which many of them expressed towards the clergy, whom they were convinced had rejected them, was very great. So much so, that a number had been completely alienated from the Church. Those people thought that they had been rejected by the Church because they were not good enough. They may have been mistaken, but many have, I know, been refused baptism on moral grounds. I have met parents whose application for the baptism of their child was declined because one partner had been divorced and remarried or because the child was illegitimate.

The effect of the Church's marriage discipline is similar. When I was the vicar of a parish, the Church of England was unable to agree to a policy on the remarriage of divorcees in church. Consequently, the parochial clergy were asked by the bishops to refuse to remarry divorcees in church, but to offer instead a Service of Prayer and Dedication, commonly, though mistakenly, referred to as a Service of Blessing. What this meant was that a couple could go and marry in the state registry office and then come to church for a service in which they affirmed their marriage vows and were prayed for.

I endeavoured to abide by this policy for a number of years, but eventually could no longer live with its inconsistency. If such a marriage was not approved by the Church, how could it be possible to affirm it in church? If it was approved, why did the Church not allow the ceremony to be performed in its buildings? The net result of this policy was that the couples who came to ask for a service were made to feel second-class citizens in comparison with those who were marrying without benefit of divorce. I felt that I was being asked to make these couples suffer for the inability of the Church of England as a whole to resolve its internal disputes. The practice was not pastorally sensitive, nor did it promote a perception of God as forgiving and loving amongst those who were on its receiving end. Consequently, I broke ranks and began remarrying divorcees in church instead of using the Service of Prayer and Dedication.

However, this did not solve the problem entirely. I was then put in the position of having to make a judgement in each individual case about whether it was appropriate or not to marry that couple in church. For example, what does it say about the Church's attitude to marriage if those involved in an adulterous relationship which resulted in the break-up of either one or both of their previous marriages are allowed to marry in church? Since I have begun working as a family therapist, I have discovered just how complex such situations can be and how difficult it is to allocate blame, even if one wished to. The Church, when it attempts to uphold a moral principle, unavoidably finds itself in the position of making such judgements about particular people as it seeks to define the boundaries of acceptable behaviour for its members. Whether its boundaries are strict or lax, it will unavoidably exclude somebody.

Preserving the Purity of the Community to Maintain the Favour of God

The drawing of boundaries around the Church has been encouraged by a tradition of interpretation, influential in both Christianity and Judaism, which links God's acceptance of the community with the maintenance of purity by its members. This is the negative side of being the Chosen People: God's requirements are more demanding of his own people than of other nations. As in the quotation from Moses in the last chapter, the continuance of God's favour is frequently presented in the Old Testament as being dependent upon obedience to his commandments, not just by the individual, but by the people as a whole. Moses threatened the Jews with a series of curses:

> However, if you do not obey the LORD your God and do not carefully follow all his commands and decrees I am giving you today, all these curses will come upon you and overtake you . . . The LORD will plague you with diseases until he has destroyed you from the land you are entering to possess . . . The LORD will cause you to be defeated by your enemies . . . The LORD will afflict you with the boils of Egypt and with tumours, festering sores and the itch, from which you cannot be cured. The LORD will afflict you with madness, blindness and confusion of mind . . . You will be pledged to be married to a woman, but another will take her and ravish her. You will build a house, but you will not live in it . . . (etc.) (Deuteronomy 28:15, 21, 25, 27–8, 30)

Judgement might fall on the whole people when one or more of them sinned. As a result large numbers of the Jewish people might die or they might be defeated in battle (e.g. Numbers 21:4–9; Joshua 7:4–5). Ultimately, long after they had occupied the Promised Land, God's punishments included the conquest of the independent Jewish kingdoms of Israel and Judah by Assyria and Babylon respectively, the destruction of the temple at Jerusalem and the deportation of the Jewish ruling class to Babylon.

Because of the dire consequences of disobedience, for those who think in this manner, God's acceptance of the community has to be preserved by the enforcement of his commands on all its members. Those who do not conform are disciplined or excluded from the community, in order to maintain its purity. This theme is prominent in the Old Testament, in which there are examples of individuals or families being executed in order to deflect God's wrath from the rest of the Hebrews. For instance, Achan *and his whole family* were stoned when it was discovered that he had stolen forbidden goods from Jericho when it was sacked by the Israelites (Joshua 7). God's punishments might include destroying many thousands of his chosen people. For example, after the Hebrews had been worshipping the golden calf, at the command of God, Moses told the Levites to arm themselves with swords and kill their brothers, friends and neighbours. The death toll was about three thousand (Exodus 32:27–8). Moses congratulated them with these chilling words: 'You have been set apart to the LORD today, for you were against your own sons and brothers, and he has blessed you this day' (Exodus 32:29) and, for good measure, after this God sent a plague amongst them. The Jewish practice of keeping God's people pure through excluding the sinner continued into New Testament times, as the stoning of Stephen (Acts 7) and the near stoning of the woman caught in adultery (John 8:1–11) indicate.

However, in the early Church the means of exclusion were not normally draconian. Although Ananias and Sapphira both dropped dead when confronted by Peter over an attempt to deceive the church (Acts 5:1–11), the usual procedure, as with Paul's command concerning an incestuous man at Corinth (1 Corinthians 5:1–13), was to cease to have anything to do with an unrepentant malefactor. This is the general advice given in St Matthew's Gospel:

'If your brother sins against you, go and show him his
fault, just between the two of you. If he listens to you, you
have won your brother over. But if he will not listen, take
one or two others along, so that "every matter may be
established by the testimony of two or three witnesses." If
he refuses to listen to them, tell it to the church; and if he
refuses to listen even to the church, treat him as you
would a pagan or a tax collector.' (Matthew 18:15–17)

Such practices were adopted by the early Church and became
institutionalised in the procedures of excommunication,
which still exist in the canon law or statutes of most churches.

After the Church became the established religion of the
Roman Empire, various forms of persecution were adopted in
order to cleanse the Church of heresy. St Augustine of Hippo,
in his dispute with the Donatists, was notable in being the first
theologian to argue for the use of secular force to eradicate
heresy (Brown, 1969, pp. 233–43). Later on, the Church developed systematic means of seeking out and expunging heresy
and disbelief, including the Inquisition and the execution of
heretics and witches. Such persecutions continued to be practised during the Reformation, alongside various other forms
of internal church discipline.

Preserving the Purity of the Contemporary Church

In recent history, the burning of heretics has ceased and attitudes to errant belief and behaviour have become more
accepting than in previous centuries. Even so, many Christians have continued to regard God's favour as being
conditional on the maintenance of the purity of the community. For example, during the Great Famine in Ireland in the
1840s:

it was widely preached, though presumably not by those
who were themselves hungry, that the Irish Famine was
the hand of God laid on a sinful people. The *Protestant
Watchman* of Dublin went a little further. It wrote to the

Prime Minister, Lord John Russell, in May 1848, telling him that his government's relief schemes were no more than a concession to Popery and a discouragement to Protestantism . . .

Fast forward to 2001 AD: The Outer Isles Presbytery of the Free Church of Scotland has stated that the visits to the Pope by the Queen and the Moderator of the Church of Scotland are responsible for the current outbreak of foot-and-mouth disease – and for the recent floods and train crashes. (Sharkey, 2001)

The theological basis for such attitudes was summed up in a Church Society pamphlet concerning the advent of AIDS, which advocated the belief that God is directly involved in the natural processes of the world, and uses them to express his anger at human sinfulness. The pamphlet listed several examples, from both the Old and the New Testaments, of God punishing people who had sinned. It came to the conclusion:

> In approaching the AIDS situation we need to recognise that God does judge in some cases, individuals and communities, here and now – cause and effect *are* his actions as much as any other natural law. In the U.K. and the U.S.A. upwards of 85% of AIDS sufferers have been homosexual, often promiscuous, practisers. The other high-risk group is the promiscuous heterosexual one. That some innocent people contract the disease through infected blood transfusions for instance, is a bitter fact of a fallen world, but not one to distract us from specifying the main cause of infection . . . to attempt to remove the element of judgment from the widespread epidemic is to close our minds to one of God's ways of speaking to the human race. Worse than that, to advocate precautions instead of repentance and renunciation of immoral behaviour is surely to compound our condemnation. We *have* been warned. (Church Society, undated, italics in original)

Although the pamphlet commends medical relief as a gift of God, the God it depicts is prepared to harm or kill the innocent in his determination to punish sexual sinners; like an army of invasion launching missiles at a city he is prepared to accept a huge amount of 'collateral damage' provided he can destroy his enemies. The God portrayed in this pamphlet does not mind hurting others in his determination to punish sexual sinners, but is strangely indifferent to much greater evils perpetrated in other spheres of life, such as politics. For some reason he allows political sinners to continue in their wickedness without let or hindrance, even though, from the human point of view, they may cause much more suffering than sexual sinners. As one American Episcopal bishop quipped, 'if AIDS is indeed the retribution from God against gay people, then shouldn't the perpetrators of terror, war, torture, and oppression in the world at least get herpes' (cited by Fortunato, 1987, p. 86).

Many Christians are particularly intolerant of those who break the rules concerning sexual behaviour, and local clergy will sometimes take the initiative to discipline or exclude members of their congregations who err in this way. For example, the Reverend Peter Irwin-Clark, a Church of England vicar, told his congregation not to associate with two members of the church who had left their spouses to live together. He based his action upon 1 Corinthians 5:11: 'But now I am writing to you that you must not associate with anyone who calls himself a brother but is sexually immoral or greedy, an idolater or a slanderer, a drunkard, or a swindler. With such a man do not even eat.' In a clarification of his injunction, he wrote to his congregation:

i)   1 Cor 5: 11 is *not* optional.
ii) It is *not* loving to offer hospitality and association to someone in rebellion against God because that will tend to confirm them in their disobedience, which leads them to eternal death.
iii) Invitations to share fellowship should be made

conditional on repentance first being fully shown . . .
(O'Neill, 1994, italics in original)

The conditional nature of church membership is stated very clearly here, and explicitly related to the threat of eternal damnation. However, exclusion is not regarded as something negative; rather, it is viewed as a positive and loving means of winning sinners back into obedience to God, and thus of ensuring their salvation, as St Paul taught (1 Corinthians 5:5).

It is not only local clergy who may seek to discipline church members. Many denominations still have formal procedures for the excommunication of those who advocate heretical views or indulge in immoral behaviour. For instance, a person who is divorced and remarries without an annulment is automatically excommunicated in the Roman Catholic Church; and in the Anglican Communion doctrinal heterodoxy may result in a priest being deprived of office. For instance, in 2002 in the Church of Ireland Andrew Furlong, the Dean of Clonmacnoise, caused much public controversy by using his personal website to deny the divinity of Christ, arguing instead that he was a moral teacher. As a result, Dean Furlong was summoned to attend a Consistory Court on the charge of heresy, but resigned on the eve of his trial.

Within the Church of England some organised pressure groups have advocated the revival of earlier strict forms of church discipline. A good example of a group promoting this way of thinking during my time in parish ministry was Action for a Biblical Witness to our Nation (ABWON), the precursor of the movement known as Reform. At its inception, its leader, the Reverend Tony Higton, circulated a letter to all the clergy of the Church of England. In it, he identified five particular targets of his campaign: Professor David Jenkins, then bishop-elect of Durham, whose orthodoxy about the resurrection and the virgin birth was in question; an inter-faith service in Newcastle Cathedral; the pro-homosexual lobby in the Church; adultery amongst the clergy; and Don Cupitt, a particularly radical theologian. His remedy for these ills was repentance, church discipline and positive biblical witness. However, if repentance was not forthcoming, Higton wanted the Church to take strong disciplinary action. Higton's letter is a clear example of the Gospel of Conditional Love. The significant words are: 'All these scandalous errors . . . can be forgiven, if they are repented of' (Higton, undated). Acceptance of the sinner only comes about *after* he or she has repented and given up the supposed sin. The alternative is discipline, in other words, punishment or rejection. The deviant one is given the choice of conformity or exclusion. Even though the bishops of the Church of England have not responded in the manner that Tony Higton demanded, they have insisted, at least in public, on certain conditions for priests to remain in office. In particular, although they have allowed homosexual laity the right of conscience to decide whether or not to live in an exclusive and committed sexually active relationship, this liberty has been denied to the clergy on the grounds of their exemplary function (Church of England, 1991, paras. 5.11–5.17, pp. 43–5).

Recently, controversy over this issue has arisen again. In June 2003 the appointment of an openly gay priest, Canon Jeffrey John, as Bishop of Reading produced a backlash that threatened to split not just the Church of England, but the worldwide Anglican Communion. Even though Canon John announced that he is now celibate, Archbishop Peter Akinola, primate of Nigeria, threatened to withdraw from communion with the Church of England if the appointment went ahead. In an interview with BBC Radio 4 he said: 'We claim we are Bible-loving Christians. We cannot be seen to be doing things clearly outside the boundaries allowable in the Bible. This is only the beginning. We would sever relationships with any-body, anywhere . . . anyone who strays over the boundaries we are out with them. It is as simple as that' (reported in the *Guardian*, 20 June 2003, p. 1). There could hardly be a clearer statement of the intention to maintain the purity of a Church by avoiding contact with Christians who stray. Subsequently, as a result of the controversy, Canon John withdrew his acceptance of the bishopric.

Immediately afterwards the controversy was re-ignited when the diocese of New Westminster in Canada approved a service of blessing for gay relationships and Canon Gene Robinson, an openly gay priest in a long-term relationship with another man, was elected as Bishop of New Hampshire and his election was subsequently confirmed by the Episcopal Church of the United States of America. At the time of writing the ongoing dispute over sexuality, especially the appointment of openly homosexual clergy, is threatening to produce schism in the Anglican Communion.

Apart from the disciplining or exclusion of individuals and attempts to control the decision-making processes of particular denominations, institutional churches or individual congregations may seek to preserve their purity by limiting as far as possible contact between their own members and those of different persuasions. An obvious example is the Exclusive branch of the Plymouth Brethren. A friend of mine, who was brought up in an Exclusive Brethren church, told me that its members were not allowed to socialise with people who did not belong and that they had to observe very strict codes of behaviour, including no drinking, smoking, dancing, cinema-going or make-up. They were also forbidden from going to university in order to prevent them from being corrupted by the secular ideas that they would be required to study there. In addition, when this group could not prevent contact with the outside world, they sought to limit the resulting contamination. Hence, my friend's father glued together the pages in his school science textbook which referred to Darwin and the theory of evolution so that he could not read them!

Such precautions may be extreme, but other churches also adopt separatist beliefs and practices. In Ireland this can be seen in the mainstream churches as well as in minority groups, as the journalist Patsy McGarry explains: 'On the macro level, "chosen people" attitudes persist and are encouraged within all denominations on the island. Most hold to the belief that they are the only true Christians. The others are not quite "proper". And each has its own theology to prove it'

(McGarry, 2001). The Irish Churches also have their own internal disciplines concerning contact with outsiders. For example, the Roman Catholic Church has long sought to separate itself from Protestants in many significant ways. In 1907 the papal decree *Ne Temere* required those of its members who married non-Catholics to bring up their children as Catholics. In the Republic of Ireland this decree resulted in a severe decline in the number of Protestants because of intermarriage. Furthermore, until recent years Roman Catholics were forbidden by their own clergy to enter Protestant churches even for weddings or funerals. Instead, they would stand in the porch during these ceremonies. This separation extended outside the religious arena into education. Until the 1970s Roman Catholics were not allowed *by their own hierarchy* to attend Trinity College Dublin, the Protestant university, without special permission. And the Catholic Church still maintains separate schools for Catholic children and insists upon this segregation in Northern Ireland, even though separate education is one of the major contributory causes of the Troubles there.

Such attitudes are not confined to Roman Catholics. The Presbyterian Church in Ireland will not invite Roman Catholic representatives to its annual General Assembly, though every other Church is invited (McGarry, 2001); and I have witnessed Anglicans refusing to take communion because the preacher at a Eucharist was Roman Catholic. A particularly extreme example of this religious segregation occurred after the Omagh bombing in 1998, in which civilian members of both the Catholic and Protestant communities were murdered whilst innocently shopping. At one town in Northern Ireland an act of remembrance was held that included no said prayers, only a space for silent reflection, because one of the Protestant ministers refused to pray with Roman Catholics. He would not even join with them in the Lord's Prayer!

Although these last examples are drawn from Ireland, where I lived for nine years, in which the Christian religion has long been closely associated with the divisions between conflictual communities, the same dynamics of inclusion and exclusion are apparent in other countries, as my other examples indicate. What varies from place to place is the precise definition of the boundary conditions of churches and the sanctions which are used to enforce them. In Ireland the conflicts and segregation are easily visible; elsewhere they are often quite subtle and more difficult to observe. However, they are almost always present and have a considerable effect on the emotional lives of churchgoers, especially through reinforcing the fear of rejection from which many already suffer because of the ambiguity in Christian teaching about whether God's love is conditional or unconditional.

Ideological Closure

The threat of exclusion or marginalisation is often implicit within the culture of a Christian church or sect. In such cases, the gospel, instead of bringing new life and freedom, tends to limit the lives of its adherents and to encourage the quest for certainty. They are likely to adopt a persona acceptable to their congregation, complying with the rules of conduct laid down by their church and accepting the definitions of truth promoted by it in a rather uncritical or even rigid manner. Such Christians will tend to turn a blind eye to those aspects of their own character or behaviour that do not conform to the group ideal and deny any doubts that they may have. They will find it very difficult to tolerate anything which puts in doubt the foundations of their faith and, therefore, they will resist facing important questions about that faith. Likewise, they will be reluctant to look at faults in the community to which they belong. If their sense of self-worth comes from their affirmation by the community, and that affirmation is itself dependent upon their acceptance of the community's values and social mores, they will find it very difficult to acknowledge that the group may be less than perfect, or that its understanding of the Christian faith is anything other than the complete truth.

42

Very often their search for belonging and acceptance gives rise in the members of a religious group to a type of intellectual restriction known as 'ideological closure'. An *ideology* is a form of belief that provides a justification for political or economic privilege. Religious belief often has an ideological role, providing ruling élites of one kind or another with a divine authority for their advantages. The identification of a political structure with the will of God enables members of privileged groups to identify themselves with those favoured by God and to justify their privileges as willed by God. When Christians use their religion to claim social or economic rights or privileges over and against others, who are regarded as in some way inferior, Christian belief is being assimilated to a particular ideological position.

The cost to Christians of adopting ideologically assimilated forms of Christian belief in order to find acceptance from both God and their own congregations may be very high because, as the educationalist John Hull explains, ideologies provide a coherent interpretation of life for those who accept them by selecting out from the confusing mass of experience certain key events or ideas around which to build their accounts of the world (Hull, 1991, p. 64). Consequently, the creation of an ideology entails a form of intellectual censorship, and membership of an ideological community requires an individual to adopt this as his or her own. In addition, the sense of certainty provided by an ideology is not secure. Because there are always alternative ways of looking at reality, there will always be a sense of anxiety or threat connected with believing in an ideology. Hull argues that this situation gives rise to what he calls *ideological closure*:

> Indeed, if it is true that human thinking is ineluctably ideological, and if ideology implies a selection of some material and a rejection of other, there will always be something intolerable upon the border of ideological orthodoxy. There will be that which resists assimilation into the ideology of the group, the unacceptable, the

alien, the intolerable. The intolerance will begin when the novelty is such as to seriously threaten the image which the group has of itself and the validity or effectiveness of its mission in the world. Ideology narrows the field of what is available to us for interpretation. In the same way, there may have been and there may still be many possible ways of interpreting the significance of the founding event or the founding lives of the community, but the ideology restricts these, so creating an orthodoxy. This act of selection leading to an orthodox interpretation we may call 'ideological closure'. (Hull, 1991, p. 65)

Ideological closure is associated with certainty and the editing out of awareness of the history by which the ideology was constructed. This is particularly the case with religions that claim to have received a revelation from God:

One of the falsifications of ideological closure is the belief that one's own Christian community is timeless and unchangeable. The ideologist does not recognize that his own thought structure is the product of a history of evolution and represents various reactions to a range of pressures including alternative ideologies within his own tradition. (Hull, 1991, p. 68)

Christian communities frequently practise ideological closure because there are so many threats to Christian belief in the contemporary world. In such cases, rather than attempting to face them and develop coherent replies to the corrosive insights of secular scholarship, Christians retreat from even acknowledging the significance of such ideas.

Ideological closure is an essential part of a form of spirituality which grows out of the identification of particular Christian communities with the People of God and is also particularly associated with covenant theology. In brief, *this spirituality short-circuits the processes of genuine spiritual growth and substitutes for them an identification of the present state of affairs with the ideal towards which Christians are striving.* When either individuals or ecclesiastical institutions adopt this spirituality, *rather than undertaking the lengthy and costly process of authentic spiritual transformation, they delude themselves that they are already in some sense what God calls them to become.* Thus, they may believe that they are more virtuous or more faithful than they actually are or that their denomination possesses a knowledge and certainty about God which it does not. Such identifications are insecure because they are constantly running up against evidence which contradicts them, and so those who are convinced by them have to push out of their awareness any events or information which might disprove them, thereby creating ideological closure.

Ideological Closure and Authoritarianism in the Church

Ideological closure in a congregation often finds its complement in an authoritarian church structure that bases its claim to authority on a version of the biblical 'Chosen People' ideology. In such ecclesiastical bodies the Church is identified in one way or another with the special favour and guidance of God. The Roman Catholic Church is an excellent contemporary example since it claims to be the one true Church and sole arbiter of Christian truth – a conviction which finds its fullest expression in the doctrine of papal infallibility – and the present Pope has been active in seeking to enforce adherence to official teaching upon its clergy and theologians. Catholic theologians have been forbidden the right to dissent from official church teaching and many individual theologians, some of great eminence, such as Hans Küng, Edward Schillebeeckx and Leonardo Boff, have been deprived of their right to teach Catholic theology. In 1990 the Congregation for the Doctrine of the Faith (formerly the Inquisition) published a document, approved by the Pope, *The Ecclesial Vocation of the Theologian*, which states that:

> To succumb to the temptation of dissent ... is to allow 'the leaven of infidelity to the Holy Spirit' to start to work ... Appealing to the obligation to one's own conscience cannot legitimate dissent ... The right conscience of a Catholic theologian presumes not only faith in the Word of God whose riches he must explore, but also love for the Church from whom he receives his mission, and respect for her divinely assisted magisterium. (Cited by Brown, 1990, p. 10)

This means that *theologians only have the right of conscience if they think what they are supposed to think!* Such a limitation on the freedom of theologians is by no means new. In reaction to the Reformation, the Council of Trent required all church officials to swear the following oath:

> I most firmly accept and embrace the Apostolic and ecclesiastical traditions and the other observances and constitutions of the Church. I also accept Sacred Scripture in the sense in which it has been held, and is held, by Holy Mother Church, to whom it belongs to judge the true sense and interpretation of the Sacred Scripture, nor will I interpret it in any other way than in accordance with the unanimous agreement of the Fathers. (Cited by Sobel, 1999, p. 72)

The response of the hierarchy of the modern Catholic Church has been equally to resort to ideological closure and an attempt to censor both the thinking and the publications of those who question its teachings. This has been necessary because the contemporary world is full of ideas that challenge these teachings and appear to put the Catholic faith in doubt.

However, this problem is by no means unique to the Roman Catholic Church. The same situation of jeopardy applies also to other conservative forms of Christianity, and traditionalist Christians of whatever denomination have been becoming more and more vocal and organised in their efforts to resist the incursions of 'liberal' views into their churches, including into the Anglican communion, and have been seeking to use the authority structures of their denominations to defend conservative beliefs and practices. The tragedy is that, if these reactionaries are allowed to succeed, those churches in which they are dominant will be condemned to exist in ever-narrower ideological enclosures in ever-increasing isolation from contemporary Western society.

The Resistance to Questioning in the Local Church

Since the ideological closure which Christian communities promote involves individuals in giving up or hiding their own perceptions of the truth in order to find emotional security in group belonging, numerous Christians have, consciously or unconsciously, surrendered their minds to the authority of their church hierarchies or what they believe to be the teaching of the Bible. Sometimes this surrender is actually described as a 'sacrifice of the intellect' and is advocated as a form of spiritual humility and virtue. Not surprisingly, those who have made such a sacrifice, or in a less extreme manner have allowed their minds to be formed by their Church's teaching, are usually considerably disturbed by any scholarship or questioning that proposes views which are not identical to those which they have been taught. Instead of exploration, they look to their church leaders to provide affirmation of their current way of life and beliefs.

Such attitudes set very severe limits on the ability of the local clergy to teach their congregations about the Christian religion in any depth or to introduce them to the conclusions of biblical scholars or of contemporary doctrinal theologians. Although some churchgoers do welcome the opportunity to learn more, and a few are genuinely searching, ordinary Christians frequently do not see the point of the questions. Far from seeking an exploration of the complexities of the Christian faith, they want their ordained ministers to affirm the truth of what they already believe.

I have frequently experienced unease at such exploration

amongst those to whom I have ministered. One of my elderly parishioners said to me after one of my sermons, 'If we are going to have all this questioning, we might as well not bother coming to church.' On another occasion, after I had given a talk, in which I had tried to explain why some people question traditional Christian beliefs, one very committed churchgoer came up to me and said, 'You have told us what we can't believe, when are you going to tell us what we can believe?' I was shaken. I had not thought that what I had said was so very negative, but that is how she had understood it. This may have been because I had spoken badly or because I had tried to say too much too quickly, but I think it was in large part because I was questioning the literal interpretation of the Bible.

The exploration of problems for belief is not only resisted by less educated churchgoers. Even trained scientists may expect teaching in church to be divorced from the findings of contemporary empirical research. One science graduate amongst my parishioners, although she personally accepted the theory of evolution, told me off for suggesting from the pulpit that Adam and Eve might not have existed; she felt I might have upset some members of the congregation. Nobody else had complained. Such attitudes are not limited to the elderly or the female: they may also be displayed by young males. When I was teaching in a theological college, many of the male theological students would object to ideas drawn from psychology or sociology which appeared in any way to put in question biblical views of morality or human nature.

Many Christians regard questioning as equivalent to un-belief. In the Church they have been taught what to believe about God and how to behave, and they have built their lives on this teaching. What they want from the Church is the assur-ance that they are loved by God, that the lives they lead are good, and that what they believe is true. What is not wanted is anything which questions that assurance. This is not because such churchgoers are incapable of thinking about new ideas. It is rather that the majority see no need for them.

They believe what they were taught and it has worked for them. It also meets their needs for affirmation. Questioning, or even thought, disturbs the quiet surface of reassurance that the Church is expected to supply, because it could suggest that their way of life or they themselves are not so acceptable to God as they wish to believe. It is, therefore, resisted.

It is also true that many churchgoers do not know enough about academic theology or modern ethical issues to understand why traditional ideas are being questioned. Lay people often are not informed about or do not understand the nature of the most important questions for contemporary theology, or why they are legitimate questions. Instead of being equipped to discuss them, they are frequently upset when anybody in authority in the Church gives anything other than the teaching with which they are familiar. They should not be blamed for this reaction; *it is the Church as an institution that is at fault for failing to educate its members.* At its best the Church has given meaning and purpose both to individuals and to society as a whole. However, the consequence of this failure to educate the laity in contemporary theology is that quite often they misunderstand what is being said and they are ill-equipped to engage constructively with modern thought.

For instance, I once talked to a Mothers' Union group about the Bishop of Durham's views. At the time Dr David Jenkins was Bishop of Durham and was very controversial for expressing what sounded like unorthodox ideas about the resurrection and the virgin birth. When I mentioned the bishop there were groans; nobody agreed with him. But after we had shared our opinions about the resurrection, I startled a number of them by pointing out that their belief in a spiritual, rather than a bodily, resurrection was not only contrary to traditional teaching, but it also had much in common with what he had been saying. They had been mistaken both in their understanding of the bishop's position and in their conviction that their own beliefs were what the Church has always taught. For them, the institutional Church represented ultimate meaning and value, and they expected its bishops not to question its teachings. It came as quite a shock to them to discover that they had themselves, without realising it, departed from the traditional teaching of the Church.

Fortunately, although there are many people in the Church who are more concerned with defending received Christian doctrine against contemporary scholarship and research than in learning from them, such churchgoers are by no means all the members of the Church. There are numerous others who long for the ecclesiastical bodies to which they belong to engage with the complexity and plurality of the everyday world they inhabit. They do not wish to live in a religious ghetto or to put their brains into cold storage every time they walk through a church's doors. Such believers are ill-served by the ordained ministers and teaching programmes of the vast majority of churches. Even so, many continue to attend more or less regularly because they recognise in the Church as a whole a genuine witness to the truth about God in Jesus Christ, and they do not want to disassociate themselves from the Christian faith and the community of believers. Staying within the Church has become more and more difficult for them in recent years because of the growing conservatism of many churches, and the increasing volume of conservative objections to even a semblance of genuine intellectual enquiry within the ecclesiastical enclaves.

Ideology in the Local Church

In spite of the criticisms I have been making, the positive value of Christianity in promoting social cohesion and in giving its adherents a sense of belonging, meaning and purpose cannot be overstated. One of the chief functions of the Christian religion throughout its history has been to provide social groups with a unifying belief system and set of moral values. Human beings are social animals: we all need to have a sense of security and to feel that we belong to a group of people by whom we are accepted. For centuries Christianity has given communities of whatever size common convictions around which they have built their lives. For many congregations it still has this function and it continues to inspire forms of behaviour which are of considerable social benefit.

The command of Christ to love our neighbours as ourselves has been especially influential in encouraging Christians to provide for the needs of others both within and beyond their immediate vicinities. Much good has resulted from this Christian teaching, including innumerable acts of unselfish, even sacrificial, care. Such concern for others is still a very frequent feature of local churches which I have often witnessed in my ministry. It has been very encouraging to me to see how churchgoers will look after one another in times of sickness, tragedy or other forms of trouble, and may also be active in local charities as fundraisers or volunteers or, more generally, involved in socially constructive ways in the local community or the workplace. Furthermore, Christian belief has been the motivation for many individuals to dedicate their lives to campaigning for the relief of poverty or fighting for social justice.

Nevertheless, local congregations may be compromised by being too closely aligned to the ideological values of the neighbourhoods they serve. There is a widespread confusion between the values of social groups and the teachings of the Christian religion. As a consequence, local churches seem often to function primarily to promote their own social and moral values which, though informed by Christianity, represent a Christianity selected and adapted to support the ideological interests of the community in which the church is placed. Ironically, whilst resisting engagement with secular knowledge through the adoption of ideological closure, ecclesiastical bodies may be very much assimilated to the secular attitudes and practices of local or national social, economic and political structures. Indeed, they may use the teaching of Christ to justify these structures and then protect these ideological beliefs, alongside more overtly religious ones, through an ideological closure which includes them both.

Most churches affirm in the name of God the way of life of those who attend them. This may also include the life of the local secular community, even though most people in the locality may rarely attend church. Consequently, the norms of a local church frequently have an ambiguous connection to the recorded teachings of Jesus of Nazareth. There is often a lack of discrimination amongst churchgoers between those aspects of supposedly Christian commitment that originate in the teachings of Jesus and the early Church and those that are part of the cultural context and social identity of the local church community. They frequently identify Jesus' teachings with the moral and political values of the social groups to which they belong and expect the local church and its clergy to be a mainstay of the values of the community. Unfortunately, when Christianity is equated with a certain type of political or ethical behaviour, it can cease to be primarily about the relationship between God and humankind and become, instead, the guarantor of the way of life of respectable society or particular social subgroups.

There is a strong desire amongst many churchgoers for the Church simply to affirm the values in which they believe. The last thing they want is any sort of challenge to the status quo, let alone a prophetic voice. As the vicar of a seaside town with a high proportion of retired people reported: 'One of our elderly ladies said to me that the best sort of ministers are those who are "always nice". They never make waves, and accept things as they are' (Petterson, 1991, p. 69). Such socially conservative expectations are usually associated with the identification of Christian belief with particular political and economic arrangements. This identification conveys 'God's approval' upon the status quo. Social conformity is seen as part of Christian commitment. In one way or another, Christ's words are edited to support the mores of the church's membership, amongst whom it becomes unacceptable to draw attention to the existence of possible contradictions between them and their own social customs. Worshippers may become very upset when any aspect of their interpretation of the gospel is questioned. I agree with John Ward, who concludes from his ministerial experience that: 'The relevance of Christ's teaching and behaviour to our daily lives is not a matter of urgency for the average conventional Christian, ordained or lay. Acceptable behaviour, as defined by contemporary society, is a much greater matter of concern for most of us' (Ward, 1989, p. 20).

When such conceptions of its purpose dominate a church, there is likely to be a conservative tone to the congregation and a strong resistance to change or to an examination of its social values. As one layman, Charles W. Tyrell, wrote: 'Contrary to modern thought, congregations would much rather hear about the widow's mite than women's ordination, or nuclear disarmament, or even Third World problems, during the time set aside for the preaching of the gospel' (Tyrell, 1988, p. 11). Of course they would. The widow's mite is a story which encourages them to be generous within the pattern of life they already know; the other subjects are more unsettling because they challenge the assumptions upon which that life is based. People will accept a challenge to do better than they are already doing, or even the denunciation of their sinfulness in general terms, provided that that challenge and that denunciation do not question the structure of their moral outlook, their political convictions or their understanding of what it means to be a Christian.

It is tempting for the clergy to collude with the expectation that nothing of any importance will be questioned within the walls of the church, because when a priest does risk challenging the basic assumptions of members of his or her congregation controversy is likely to result. I discovered how easily this can happen when in my parish magazine I raised some fairly mild questions about the reforms of the National Health Service being proposed by the Conservative government of the time. About half my congregation were Conservative party supporters, and a number were upset by what they regarded as my 'illegitimate involvement of religion in politics'. The local Conservative Member of Parliament was none too pleased either. Paradoxically, a priest is not expected to question the political authorities, even though Christ was undoubtedly a non-conformist who challenged the kind of conventional religiosity which functions as a substitute for meeting the true demands of righteousness and justice.

The expectation that the Church will support the existing social and political structures applies as much at the national as at the local level. A good example is the relationship between the Conservative government of Margaret Thatcher and the Church of England. This was the background to most of my parochial ministry in England, and was, for me, a constant source of annoyance, since much that the Tory government was doing seemed to me to be opposed to social justice. The Conservatives called for the Church to give a moral lead to the nation, but defined the nature of this morality in very narrow individualistic terms. For example, Mr Graham Riddick, a Conservative Member of Parliament, asked in the House of Commons:

> When are we going to get some real leadership from the Church? I should like to hear Church leaders speak about the need for individuals to exercise responsibility over the way they run their lives. When are we going to hear the Archbishops of Canterbury and York calling for a moral regeneration of the country, and telling us what is right and wrong, and urging parents to exercise more responsibility and discipline over their children? (Reported in the *Church Times*, 17 March 1989)

Such a moral lead from the Church would have fitted in very well with the Conservative government's stress on the individual. Ironically, however, when the Church sought to give a moral lead, which involved criticising the government for neglect of the inner cities, the government was highly aggressive in its attitude towards the Church. The *Faith in the City* report (Church of England, 1985), which contained the Church's criticisms, was branded by some Tories as Marxist, even though its ethical basis was the Christian teaching on social justice whose origins go back to the prophets of the eighth century BC.

The Ideological Assimilation of Christian Belief

The Tory government's belief that the Church of England should support a socially conservative policy is understandable when it is remembered that the Church of England originated as an established Church supporting King Henry VIII's, and later Queen Elizabeth I's, political programmes. Its historical association with the ruling-class is visible in almost every parish church and cathedral, in which numerous memorials are found to the local gentry and aristocracy. This connection can be seen very clearly in the nineteenth-century novels of, for example, Jane Austen and Anthony Trollope in which the parochial clergy function as an extension of the landowning-class, and the privileges of the local squire are enshrined in his possession of a special pew and, often, the right to appoint the parson. Church members were expected to accept this highly hierarchical organisation of society as well as the legally sanctioned forms of Christian belief defined by the Thirty-Nine Articles of Religion in *The Book of Common Prayer*.

Churches are often the repositories of ancient regimental colours and may contain special chapels dedicated as memorials to the local regiment. I came across a good example of this in Chester Cathedral. The following is taken from a notice describing the South Transept chapels:

> Facing you is the chapel of the Cheshire Regiment dedicated to St George. On the reredos is a carving of St George slaying the Dragon. Hanging in a line at the back of all four Chapels are the Colours of the Cheshire regiment . . . On the left is the chapel of St Oswald, King of Northumbria 633–41. The reredos was designed by the stained-glass artist C. E. Kempe, and carved in Oberammergau. In the centre is St Oswald. On the side he erects

the wooden cross before which he prayed for victory on the eve of the battle against the heathen, which won him the Kingdom of Northumbria. On the other side he dies a martyr's death in battle near Oswestry.

This notice makes no comment on the paradox of a Christian associating the cross with victory in battle, let alone using it, as St Oswald and numerous other Christians did, as a military standard. Nor does it point out the strangeness of calling St Oswald's death a martyrdom because the enemy he fought against was 'heathen'. However, such an assimilation of death in battle to Christ's death on the cross is very common in war memorials, as in this chapel.

A similar association between military violence and Christ's death is also found in Ireland. As Patrick McGlinchey says: 'One of the most disturbing aspects of the Irish conflict is the extent to which religion has been used to legitimise the taking up of arms' (McGlinchey, 1996, p. 36). This was true of both sides in the struggle for independence from Britain. Amongst Republicans, it is found most notably in the work of Patrick Pearse, who was executed after the Easter rising in 1916. McGlinchey has identified four components of the 'mystical nationalism' that Pearse created and which inspired many a republican 'rebel': the identification of patriotism with holiness; the identification of the death of the patriot with the death of Christ; the viewing of the Irish as a Messianic people; and, the glorification of bloodshed and violence (McGlinchey, 1996, pp. 37–8). For Pearse, the death of the patriot is equivalent to Christ's sacrifice: 'As the blood sacrifice of Christ procured salvation for the world, so the patriot, by the shedding of his blood, can free the captive people' (McGlinchey, 1996, p. 38). In addition, in Pearse's thought 'the sufferings of Christ become a metaphor for the condition of the Irish people' (McGlinchey, 1996, p. 38).

The Unionist Protestants equally saw their cause as backed by God, but in their case, drawing on the tradition of the Covenanters of the sixteenth and seventeenth centuries, they had 'a sense of being a special group that has been set apart by God and given the land of Ulster as a form of promised land' (McGlinchey, 1996, p. 40). They believed that 'Home rule is Rome rule'. The threat of being incorporated into a predominantly Roman Catholic state meant a threat to the very existence of their Protestant faith and, thus, of their salvation. Hence, they were determined to fight to prevent it from happening. The very name 'Covenanters' indicates that those who belonged to this movement regarded themselves as being the contemporary successors of the chosen people with whom God made his covenant.

The arrogation to themselves of the identity of the 'Chosen People' and its use as an ideological support for national ambitions is by no means limited to Ulster Protestants. It has had many incarnations, not least in the development of English identity and of the British Empire. Such identifications depend on the use of what is known as *typology*, which is the association of a present political or social situation with one found in the Bible. This is more than a simple drawing of parallels; rather, it carries with it the idea that the present state of affairs is equivalent to that in the past and that God is involved with it in the same way as he was in the past. Thus, in the case of the adoption of a 'Chosen People' typology, God may be expected to behave towards the new Chosen People in the same way as he did towards the Jews, those originally chosen. They will receive the same benefits as the Jews did – God's protection and the donation of a 'Promised Land' – but they will also stand under the same threat of judgement and eventual rejection if they do not obey him.

Such a 'Chosen People Typology' is easily assimilated to ideology. A good example of the use of typology to support the ideological assimilation of religion to the interests of a dominant race is found in the coronation service of Queen Elizabeth II in 1953. Clifford Longley provides a revealing analysis of its meaning:

At the core of this ideology . . . is the idea of chosenness,

57

a covenant based on a typological relationship to history recorded in the Old Testament. The assumption was that English history would happen on parallel lines to ancient Israelite history, so that what was true of the latter would also be, in some sense, true of the former. The parallels would not always be obvious. Interpretations would differ. But by and large, if England was unfaithful to God, God would chastise it by sending defeat and misfortune; if England was faithful, God would reward it with victory, peace and prosperity. Provided the covenant was intact, at times of great danger God would intervene. (Longley, 2002, pp. 52–3)

The use of typological parallels between the present political order and aspects of the biblical depiction of God's relationship with his people, and of an identification between a particular race or state and the chosen people of God, is by no means exceptional. Longley argues that it provides the foundation for both English and American national identity. It is also, for example, found amongst the Protestants of Northern Ireland (as we have already seen) and the Afrikaaners of South Africa.

However, the idea of chosenness is not only used to support dominant racial groups. The Hebrews, the original chosen people, moved from being slaves to being successful conquerors of a fertile land. An identification with the chosen people may also be used by underdogs in their struggle for freedom. This was the case amongst black slaves in the United States and continued after emancipation to provide inspiration for the civil rights movement. As Longley explains: 'In the theory of biblical typology, it was as a people – akin to the Israelite people in the Old Testament – that black people were persecuted, and as a people therefore that they would be liberated (from "bondage in Egypt" etc.), with God's help but by their own efforts' (Longley, 2002, p. 255).

In one way or another, the use of Christian typology to promote political power has been ubiquitous throughout the

Christian era and, beginning with the Emperor Constantine, the identification of a ruler with Christ has also been common. Constantine made Christianity the official religion of the Roman Empire, and redesigned Christian iconography in the image of the pagan Emperor cult:

> According to this imperial theology there is one transcendent God who is the 'Supreme Sovereign'; there is one divine Logos or Word of God who governs the universe, and who is indistinguishable in essence from the one God; and there is one human monarch who governs earth as God's representative. The last in this succession is, of course, Constantine, who regards himself as the image on earth of the Logos, 'deriving his imperial authority from above'. (Fiddes, 2000, pp. 63–4)

This kind of identification is given concrete form in the twelfth-century royal crown of Hungary:

> On the upper front of the crown facing outwards is a portrait, Christ Pantocrator, Christ the world-ruling Logos. As his subjects approach the king, they see above his human face the divine face of Christ. The heavenly king sanctions the rule of the king on earth, who thus wears the face of Christ and has become one with him. Political theology is incarnate in gold. (Fiddes, 2000, p. 65)

The identification of the monarch with Christ has been very common in the history of Christian monarchies and has served to justify the sovereign's absolute authority. Coronation services make this link overt in the act of anointing with oil the sovereign who, thereby, becomes 'the Lord's anointed', another common typological association dating back to Samuel's anointing of Saul, the first king of Israel (1 Samuel 10:1). In this ceremony and its accompanying typology the doctrine of the divine right of kings, which cost Charles I of England and Scotland his head, found its justification.

The tendency to assimilate Christianity to its political context is not limited to monarchies or countries in which the

Church is established by law. A good contemporary example of such a case is the United States of America where, although officially and constitutionally there is a division between Church and State, in practice the Christian faith is often used to support the political order. Despite its constitutional prohibition of a state religion, the United States has a *de facto* civic religion in which the ideological values of democracy, natural rights and freedom are identified with and justified by the Christian religion (Clark, 2001). This was very clear in the memorial service held in Washington for the victims of the attacks on 11 September 2001. Watching the service from the initial procession of military colours through the singing of 'America' and the President's address, it was often unclear who was being worshipped, God or America. In this 'act of worship' Christianity was implicitly promoted as a support for the American 'democratic' political ideology, which is also very closely associated with neo-liberal capitalism and American dominance of world politics and economics. Christianity, in this context, justifies democratic capitalism and economic imperialism, just as in the Byzantine era it justified the rule of the Emperor. This identification of America with freedom and democracy and, thus, with goodness and the favour of God was made even more evident in the speeches of President George W. Bush in the run-up to the Iraq War. He frequently depicted America as a beacon of freedom and goodness fighting against the evil of Saddam Hussein and terrorism. These attitudes disclose the existence of a fundamental typological association of the American people with the chosen people of God (Longley, 2002).

In contrast, in contemporary South America, Christianity in the form of liberation theology encourages the identification of a different people with the ancient Israelites, namely, the poor; and it supports their struggle for social justice against the rich. Liberation theologians claim that God has 'a preferential option for the poor' (Gutierrez, 1999, p. 27), and that the poor have privileged access to the truth about God. As Professor Christopher Rowland explains:

What some liberation theologians are claiming is that the vantage point of the poor is particularly, and especially, the vantage point of the crucified God and can act as a criterion for theological reflection, biblical exegesis and the life of the Church. The poor are the means whereby the Church can learn to discern the truth, direction and content of its mission, and they can assure the Church of being the place where the Lord is found. (Rowland, 1999, pp. 6–7)

Liberation theologians frequently use the story of the exodus of the Hebrew slaves from Egypt to support the idea that God is on the side of the poor in their struggle against the rich, thereby making the poor functionally equivalent to the Jews and claiming for them the same relationship of divine favour and intervention that the Jews enjoyed. This form of Christian belief is heavily influenced by Marxist thought and has been used to support resistance to oppressive regimes, many of which, ironically, are supported by the United States. Confusingly, in different parts of the contemporary world Christianity is adopted as an ideological underpinning by both capitalist and Marxist political movements which are in conflict with each other.

It seems clear from these examples that the form which the Christian religion takes in any particular cultural context is liable to be heavily influenced by the economic and power relationships within the societies in which it exists. We may conclude that Christianity advocates significantly different political and economic arrangements in different times and places because it is to a considerable degree assimilated to the ideological concerns of the communities in which it flourishes. The Christian religion has often become a badge of community membership. As a consequence, when someone wishes to join a Christian church she or he is very likely to be expected to accept a version of Christian belief that is to a large degree assimilated to its ideological context, including the social structures and mores that it supports. Failure to do so may result in ecclesiastical marginalisation or exclusion.

CHAPTER THREE

The Cost of Belonging

The Formation of the Christian Complex

We have seen how Christianity is almost always assimilated to ideology and is used to support particular economic and political arrangements, and how the boundary conditions of local congregations often mirror the conditions for social inclusion of the ideological communities within which they are placed. Even so, churches vary enormously in the extent to which they are prepared to tolerate aberrant behaviour amongst their members. Where the faith of a congregation is strongly influenced by ideological closure or the Gospel of Conditional Love, acceptance of moral or doctrinal difference is likely to be low. As we have seen, this means that, in order to belong to such churches, members have to deny those aspects of their beliefs, characters and desires which are not approved of by their fellows. Wherever strict boundary conditions exist churchgoers, if they are to find approbation and a sense of belonging in their religious communities, are required to fit themselves into a belief system or way of life that may not accommodate significant aspects of their personalities. This has psychological consequences for the individual which may be very severe and which we will now examine.

There are numerous different schools of contemporary

psychology with differing theoretical understandings and associated therapeutic practices. They all have something to contribute to an understanding of the responses of believers and others to the presentation of God's love in the Christian religion. However, for our purposes I am going to draw primarily on the Object Relations and Jungian schools of psychology. The former was founded by Melanie Klein, a follower of Sigmund Freud. The latter was founded by Carl Jung, who was also at one point very close to Freud, but eventually broke with him and developed a significantly different understanding of human psychology. Whereas Klein's psychology concentrates on the effect the earliest relationship of the mother and baby has upon emotional development, Jung's is more concerned with the second half of life. Despite differences of language and emphasis, the two schools are in many ways complementary, and numerous psychotherapists and analysts use them in combination as the basis of their work. In addition, these schools have both been used extensively to interpret religious experience from a psychological perspective. I believe that they provide very suggestive interpretative tools for our present purposes which help us to understand why it is that Christians may sacrifice aspects of their own identity in order to belong to the Church.

Central to Klein's description of infant experience is the emotion of anxiety. This arises from the trauma of birth and of occasions when a baby's needs are not immediately fulfilled; in other words, experiences of hunger, physical discomfort, pain or loss. Such experiences are not understood by infants, who do not yet have the resources of language and rationality. They cannot make sense of such distress, which is simply experienced as threatening. Even in adults a sense of incomprehensible threat gives rise to anxiety; all the more so in babies whose first emotional reactions are dominated by the contrast between feelings of anxiety and feelings of well-being arising from the satisfactions of feeding, holding and physical comfort, and by anger or hatred when such comforts are not available or are withdrawn (Klein 1959/1988, pp. 248–9).

Klein's theories about early child development illuminate the anxiety that is experienced by many Christians in their relationship with God, which appears to be the equivalent to the existential anxiety suffered by an infant whose needs are not met and who is faced with the experience of apparent abandonment to a hostile world. All of us have had this type of experience in our earliest months, though for most help did come quickly enough to prevent permanent crippling emotional damage. Nevertheless, the memory of this anxiety remains with us, even if only unconsciously, and the feelings of fear, loss and abandonment can be revived by distressing events in adult life. Those who have not established a secure sense of themselves as being loved and acceptable human beings may staunch their inner insecurity through religious belief, which becomes part of their psychological defences against anxiety and other disturbing emotions.

Psychological defences originate in infancy. Infants have not yet developed the capacity to make sense of negative emotions and so they have to prevent themselves from being overwhelmed by what they feel. The way in which they do this is to use a range of unconscious and automatic defence mechanisms, one of the chief of which is splitting. *Splitting* refers to the separation of different aspects of a person from each other in an infant's mind, for instance, the mother when she is giving loving attention from the mother when she is emotionally distant. What this means is that the mother who is close and nurturing is experienced as if she were a different person from the mother who appears uncaring. Consequently, the nurturing mother is not blamed by the baby for the failures of the neglectful mother, and she is likely to be idealised by her baby. Likewise, infants may internally split their own love from their own anger and, thereby, experience themselves as feeling only love towards their mothers, and their anger as if it were an external and malevolent presence attacking them. Such a psychological configuration is quite common in adults as well as children. Many adults are significantly unaware of their own negative emotions towards other people or themselves and constantly either blame or feel criticised by others.

Splitting or dissociation (the term more commonly adopted by Jungians) is an unconscious means of defence which we all make use of to protect our conscious minds from becoming aware of emotions which would be too disturbing to handle. Consequently, we may 'forget' all manner of experiences which are associated with strong and difficult emotions. If too much of this kind of dissociation happens within a personality it may result in the development of a *neurosis*, which is a state of internal division in which different parts of an individual's personality are in unconscious conflict with each other. The individual concerned is not aware of the contents of the conflict, suffering instead from the symptoms that result, such as anxiety states, delusional states, depression, obsessions, compulsions, phobias, hysteria, or feelings of meaninglessness and worthlessness. The distress caused by such symptoms may lead those afflicted to enter psychotherapy.

In this respect, religion may provide a certain benefit to its adherents insofar as it assists them to cope with anxiety and other troubling emotions and to feel loved, but it may also have negative consequences and itself be responsible for caus-ing psychological disturbance or preventing its resolution. Jung claimed that Christianity as a religion is psychologically unhealthy because it promotes spiritual practices based on an ideal of *perfection* which tend to create a neurotic split in the psyches of Christians (Jung, 1951/1968). In other words, it encourages a dissociation of the personality of the believer or prevents the resolution of any that already exist. As he saw it, the Christian ideal is to be perfect, in other words, to imitate Christ, to be totally obedient to God, selfless, loving towards others and prepared to sacrifice oneself, even to the point of death. Traditionally this ideal has been linked with asceticism, the denial of instinctual desires, especially sexual ones, and the mortification of the body, even including self-flagellation and starvation.

Like Freud and Klein, Jung distinguished between

conscious and unconscious aspects of the personality. From his perspective, an individual is only aware of a part of his or her own self; much remains unconscious and therefore unrecognised, as he described it: 'Consciousness is like a surface or a skin upon a vast unconscious area of unknown extent. We do not know how far the unconscious rules because we simply know nothing of it' (Jung, 1935/1977, p. 8, para. 11). He regarded the aim of psychological growth to be *wholeness* or *completeness*, an ideal state of psychic integration in which there is a co-operative relationship between the conscious and unconscious minds (Jung, 1951/1968). Jung argued that the achievement of psychological wholeness was inconsistent with perfection because the pursuit of perfection produced an internal conflict between the conscious and unconscious parts of the personality (Jung, 1951/1968, pp. 68–71, paras. 123–6), a conflict which is associated with various symptoms of psychological distress, ranging in severity from individual unhappiness, lack of fulfilment and neurosis through mental illness to widespread social disruption (Neumann, 1973).

I believe that Jung was correct about the fundamental psychological split at the core of the normative teaching about heaven and hell in Christianity, and its capacity to produce or encourage the development of neurotic forms of psychological functioning in believers. However, I do not think that his distinction between wholeness and perfection goes far enough in describing the possible psychological consequences of Christian faith and practice. Mainstream Christianity is very frequently, perhaps inevitably, implicated in a form of psychological and social functioning that I call *the Christian complex*. In adopting this term I am not denying that there are other complexes associated with and encouraged by Christian teaching and practice. However, because it is so common and is rooted in and sustained by the doctrine that there is a final judgement at which all people will be allocated for eternity to heaven and hell, and because this belief is at the heart of what is normally understood to be orthodox Christian belief, I believe that I am justified in calling it 'the' rather than 'a' Christian complex. It is a *necessary* consequence of this doctrine and will, therefore, *inevitably* accompany orthodox Christianity, even if not all practising Christians develop this complex as individuals.

Probably, the best-known examples of complexes are Sigmund Freud's Oedipus and mother complexes, and Alfred Adler's inferiority complex. Jung used the theory of complexes to account for the results of association experiments he undertook with his patients. Subjects were given lists of a hundred words to which they had to respond spontaneously with other words. Delays in their response times and other particular types of interference in their responses were found to indicate the presence of a complex (Jung, 1973). According to Jung:

> *Complexes* are psychic fragments which have split off owing to traumatic influences or certain incompatible tendencies. As the association experiments prove, complexes interfere with the intentions of the will and disturb the conscious performance; they produce disturbances of memory and blockages in the flow of associations; they appear and disappear according to their own laws; they can temporarily obsess consciousness, or influence speech and action in an unconscious way. In a word, complexes behave like independent beings, a fact especially evident in abnormal states of mind. (Jung, 1937/1969, p. 121, para. 253; italics added)

These 'psychic fragments' are formed by the organisation of various unconscious parts of the personality around a kernel associated with a particular emotion. This kernel may be a past traumatic event, a part of the personality that has been denied expression in social life or some undeveloped potential that has not yet become conscious. As the Jungian analyst Jolande Jacobi describes it:

> The complex consists first of a 'nuclear element', a

vehicle of meaning, which is usually unconscious and autonomous, hence beyond the subject's control, and second of the manifold associations linked with it and marked by the same emotional tone; these in turn draw their content partly from original personal disposition and partly from outside experience. (Jacobi, 1973, p. 36)

In his later work, Jung came to believe that at the core of each complex lies an archetype, an inherited instinctual element of the human psyche which gives rise to basic patterns of behaviour and image formation. However, we do not need to accept Jung's theory of archetypes in order to make use of his theory of complexes; after all he developed the latter before the former and psychologists who are not Jungians also make use of the theory. What is important for us here is to recognise that there is at the heart of every complex some split-off aspect of the personality that attracts to itself other aspects to form a conglomeration which lives a relatively independent life in the unconscious of an individual, as a partial or fragmentary personality. As Jung said, 'The complex is not under the control of the will and for this reason it possesses the quality of psychic autonomy' (Jung, 1928/1966a, p. 131, para. 266), which is why complexes are problematic; they may cause those who are affected by them to act in ways which they would not consciously choose and which may be actually harmful to themselves or other people.

Even so, complexes are a part of normal psychology. We all have them. They are not in themselves a sign of psychopathology. The failure to acknowledge the existence of a complex is what creates problems, because this blindness enables the complex to interfere with the conscious intentions of the personality in a potentially destructive manner. Since complexes are unconscious they are expressed indirectly through neurotic symptoms. For example, those who suffer from a mother complex have not yet freed themselves sufficiently from an emotional dependence upon their mothers or from the feelings about them, whether positive or negative, that were appropriate when they were small children. As a result, they will at times respond emotionally to other people as if they were their mothers, and may unconsciously attempt to get them to care for them in a motherly way and blame them when they do not. Their behaviour in relation to these persons will have much in common with that of a child towards his or her mother. Or, they may be excessively motherly themselves. Confusingly, they may at the same time be able to behave in normally adult ways for much of their lives and may be competent at their work. Even so, when for some reason the complex is activated in particular circumstances or relationships, they act emotionally like children not like grown-ups.

On occasion, even though complexes are normally considered parts of an individual's psychology, a person's relationship with the outside world may be responsible for the formation of a complex. This point is very important in the creation of the Christian complex. As Murray Stein explains:

> Usually one considers complexes to be 'personal'. And it is true that most complexes are generated in a person's specific life history and belong strictly to the individual. But there are also family and social complexes. Such complexes belong no more to the individual than a disease belongs to an individual. It belongs to a collective, and the individual 'catches' it. This means that in society many people are similarly wired, psychologically speaking. People who grow up in the same families or extended kinship groups or traditional cultures share a great deal of this common unconscious structure . . . We can think here of a cultural layer of the unconscious, a sort of cultural unconscious. It is personal in the sense that it is acquired in the individual's lifetime, but it is collective because it is shared with a group. The unconscious, at this level, is structured by larger cultural patterns and attitudes, and these end up influencing the

individual's conscious attitudes and the more unique complexes within a nexus of unconscious cultural assumptions. (Stein, 1998, pp. 46–7)

The emotional core of the Christian complex is the combination of a desire to be loved with a fear of rejection. The interaction of the desire of believers for the love and acceptance of God with the conditions laid down for church membership, alongside the fear of ultimate rejection, creates the circumstances within which the Christian complex occurs. This is why it is a frequent feature of the modes of relationship practised within the Church as well as of the internal lives of individual believers. In Jungian terms, it exists in the cultural unconscious and is passed on to individuals through the interaction of a person's emotional needs with Christian education and socialisation.

The Christian Complex as a System

Because the Christian complex functions as a social complex it is not confined to personal psychology; it not only produces emotional and behavioural symptoms in individuals, but also gives rise to a series of interconnected actions and attitudes at the social as well as the individual level. The manner in which the Christian complex is communicated to individuals through the Christian groups to which they belong may be illuminated by regarding the complex as a system:

> Very simply, *a system* is any unit structured on feedback (Bateson 1972). More fully, a system is seen as existing when we can identify an entity made up of a set of interacting parts which mutually communicate with and influence each other. The parts are connected so that each part influences and is influenced by each other part. In turn these continually interacting parts are connected together such that they display identifiable coherent patterns. These overall patterns are not simply reducible to the sum of the actions of the individual's parts – a system is more than simply the sum of its composite parts. It is

the observed pattern that connects the parts in a coherent and meaningful way. (Dallos & Draper, 2000, p. 24, italics added)

A system is a dynamic form of relationship in which there is a constant interaction between the constituent parts and the world outside the system. All parts of a system are connected to every other part and a change in any one of them will affect all of the others. A good example is the human body in which the functioning of each organ is influenced by the functioning of the whole body, i.e. every other organ, and vice versa. In social systems there is a similar exchange of influence between the different 'organs', be they individual people, groups or institutions.

From a systemic standpoint, the network of interconnected behaviours, beliefs and emotions that constitutes the Christian complex operates both within and between individuals. Indeed, children and converts are inducted into it through the external practices of the Church and its members, and learn to internalise the behaviours, beliefs and emotions connected with it. Consequently, because churches are normatively assimilated to the collective context in which they are placed, the conditions for acceptance, included in individuals' versions of the complex, generally incorporate many aspects of the social mores and ideologies of the cultures and societies to which church members belong.

Systems have a tendency to stay the same, a feature which theorists call *homeostasis*. When something changes, the dynamics of the system attempt to bring it back to the state in which it began, like a thermostat controlling a house's central heating system. Because the Christian complex functions as a system, a change in one part of it has implications for every other. The systemic nature of the Christian complex is important because the complicated interactions that keep it in existence have a conservative effect. It is very difficult to change any of a system's elements in any significant way because of the constraining influence of the other elements.

71

This is one reason why change in the Church, which is itself a huge social system, gives rise to so much resistance and can be so painfully slow.

The Christian Persona

We have seen that the Christian complex is created and maintained in the interaction between the human need to be loved, and its associated fear of rejection with Christian teaching about the love of God, and the behavioural expectations of local congregations upon their members. Individuals may use the Christian religion in two related ways to meet their desire for love and acceptance. The first is by seeking love directly from God and the second is by looking for it from the Christian community, the Church. In theory, it is possible to have a relationship with either God or the Christian community that does not involve the Christian complex. However, in many people the complex becomes active because their often unconscious fear of rejection leads them, in one way or another, to sacrifice an aspect of their individual identity that is essential to their integrity. They conform to an ideal of Christian virtue, or the commands of a spiritual leader, or the mores or ideological closure of a Christian group that are unduly restrictive of their personalities and injurious to their psychological well-being. Jung's distinction between 'the ego' and 'the persona' is helpful in understanding how this happens.

The centre of consciousness and those aspects of the personality with which it is associated Jung called 'the ego' (Jung, 1923/1971, Vol. 6, p. 425, para. 706). The *ego* is the centre of that part of his or her self of which an individual is aware, the 'I am', the centre of the conscious core of a person, but not the whole of someone's identity; there are always other characteristics of which the ego remains in ignorance. Jung also recognised an aspect of the personality concerned with relating the ego to the outer world of human society. This is what he called the *persona*, a term which in ancient Greek society 'meant the mask worn by actors to indicate the role they played' (Jung, 1928/1966b, p. 157, para. 245). As Jung describes it: 'The persona is a complicated set of relations between the individual consciousness and society, fittingly enough a kind of mask, designed on the one hand to make a definite impression upon others, and, on the other, to conceal the true nature of the individual' (Jung, 1928/1966b, p. 193, para. 305). The adaptations that a person has to make in order to function within society create the persona, as Jung says:

> Fundamentally the persona is nothing real: it is a compromise between the individual and society as to what a man should appear to be. He takes a name, earns a title, exercises a function, he is this or that. In a certain sense all this is real, yet in relation to the essential individuality of the person concerned it is only a secondary reality, a compromise formation, in making which others have a greater share than he. The persona is a semblance, a two-dimensional reality, to give it a nickname. (Jung, 1928/1966b, p. 158, para. 246)

Everybody needs to develop a persona, and much of the process of bringing up children is concerned with its formation in order to make them, in the words of Jungian analyst Erich Neumann, 'clean about the house' (Neumann, 1973, p. 38). Because no one can live an uninhibited instinctual life in a structured and civilised society, the persona is a social necessity.

The persona is created through the use of the psychological mechanisms of suppression and repression, which were first identified by Sigmund Freud. Freud's psychology is concerned with the means by which individuals balance the demands of internal instinctual drives, especially sexuality, against parental and societal restraints and the demands of external reality. He used the ideas of suppression and repression to explain how unacceptable aspects of the personality are managed by individuals so that they may consciously conform to the demands of society. *Suppression* is the *conscious* process of refusing to live out those elements of the personality that are not in accord with a personal or social ideal. For example, a monk suppresses his sexual desires in order to live a celibate life, and a girl may suppress her intelligence because she believes men will not be attracted to a woman who is intellectual. Suppression is at the heart of all forms of asceticism and is often a considerable moral achievement, accompanied as it is by the suffering that arises from the frustration of desire (Neumann, 1973, pp. 34–5).

Alternatively, unacceptable aspects of the personality may be repressed. *Repression* is the process by which people forget things about themselves (e.g. memories, desires, thoughts, feelings, frightening and traumatic experiences) and then forget that they have forgotten them (Freud, 1901/1960). People who have repressed aspects of themselves genuinely do not realise that those traits are part of themselves. Such traits have suffered a fate similar to that of 'unpersons' in George Orwell's novel *Nineteen Eighty-Four* (1954). In that novel people who had fallen foul of the totalitarian regime of Big Brother had the records of their existence destroyed. However, the directives ordering this eradication to take place referred to these individuals as 'unpersons', as if they had *never* existed and there had been an error in the records.

When people repress painful aspects of their experience or self-knowledge the end result is that, for them, it is as if whatever they have hidden from themselves never existed. However, the problem is that such features of themselves do continue to exist, but out of the conscious awareness of the individuals concerned. Others in their vicinity, relatives, friends and colleagues, may be only too aware of what they have repressed, because their behaviour gives repeated evidence of those aspects of character of which the repressors have ceased to be aware, for example, overreactions, egocentricity, passive aggression, irresponsibility or power-seeking.

The Christian Neurosis

As we have seen, within the Church it is very common for

believers to be expected by their co-religionists, and indeed by non-Christians, to conform to the standards proclaimed by Christian teaching or, at least, not to appear to contravene them to any serious degree. There is often a strong internal group expectation of conformity placed upon members of Christian congregations. In other words, churchgoers are expected to adopt a persona which is in accord with the group norms. Not to do so will result in criticism, social discomfort, marginalisation and, possibly, exclusion. Those parts of their personalities that come under condemnation from religious teaching or social expectations and which, therefore, church-goers cannot face in themselves or reveal to others, are likely to be suppressed. Through this psychological mechanism unacceptable aspects of their characters are denied conscious expression and individuals, by adopting a persona acceptable to their fellow believers, are able to achieve social integration and take part in corporate and religious life. Christians often resort to such suppression in order to achieve a good con-science. This is encouraged by traditional forms of Christian education and socialisation.

Some years ago a French psychiatrist, Pierre Solignac, pro-duced a book called *The Christian Neurosis* (Solignac, 1982). Commenting from a psychiatric and Freudian perspective, he presented numerous case histories of those, predominantly priests and religious, who had been harmed psychologically by the suppression associated with traditional Catholic edu-cation, especially in the area of sexuality. Solignac's concern is with the manner in which the Christian faith has been taught, and the kinds of psychological development it has promoted in its adherents. I myself, and many psychotherapists of my acquaintance in Ireland, have frequently come into contact with clients whose emotional development has been similarly blighted by a traditional Catholic upbringing.

It seems clear that, when the Christian gospel has been taken to set before believers a very high ideal of selfless and self-denying behaviour, it has frequently resulted in neurotic symptoms amongst them. Love of self has been described as sinful and strongly discouraged in favour of love of neighbour, but the inculcation of selflessness in childhood has occurred before the child has had sufficient of his or her needs for affirmation and love met in order to establish an adequate degree of individual identity, i.e. an ego. Often believers have sacrificed themselves before they have developed a self to sacrifice, and this has been achieved not just by suppression, but in large measure by repression. An education which encourages too much suppression is highly likely to provoke its victims also to use repression extensively. This is because they cannot conform to what they are commanded by acts of will alone and, thus, are unable to achieve a good conscience without resorting to repression. Consequently, they may cease to be aware of those aspects of their personalities and actions that do not fit into the pattern of life prescribed by authority figures and inculcated by education. When those authority figures are Christian ones and that education is carried out by agents of the Church, the Christian religion has become a vehicle for what Solignac terms 'the sanctification of oppression' (Solignac, 1982). Such oppression may continue in the lives of adults, if they are subjected to forms of spirituality which emphasise self-sacrifice in a manner that prevents the mature functioning of the ego.

Christians who have been on the receiving end of such sanctified oppression are likely not to have developed a strong enough internal basis of self-regard in order to practise living a life for others without reinforcing the injury to their psychological growth inflicted by their education. Paradoxically, it is only when we have built up a strong enough sense of our own self-worth that we become able genuinely to love others for themselves. Otherwise, we are very likely to use even our overtly loving actions as means to compensate for our inner lack of self-love. Thus, those who spend much of their time doing good works for others may, actually, be unconsciously trying to prove to themselves that they are of value by serving others. Alternatively, they may be giving to others the caring that they are themselves unconsciously longing to receive.

Rather than a truly compassionate heart, their 'loving' activities may be covering up an emotional inability truly to value or look after themselves. In a similar manner, those who have been ordained or entered the religious life, often in their late teens, may never have developed a mature ego. The spiritual disciplines that they have been expected to undertake, especially those associated with obedience, have treated them like children, denying them adult responsibility for their own lives. It is hardly surprising, therefore, that many Christians have developed psychological disorders and ended up as patients of Dr Solignac or his colleagues.

The Psychology of the Good Child

Nevertheless, it must be emphasised that not all children who are brought up as Christians are subjected to religious oppression; a Christian education may be benign and constructive. Even so, it will always inculcate certain Christian convictions in those who receive it which have the potential to encourage unhealthy forms of psychological splitting. In normal psychological development children come to identify with the values and beliefs of their carers. This is necessary because, before they can develop their own individuality, they need to have sufficient strength of character or, in psychological language, 'ego strength', and this is normally achieved through identification with the code of behaviour and opinions, and hence the approval, of their parents. Only at adolescence, as they seek to establish a more independent adult identity, do most children begin seriously to question their parents' views, if they ever do at all. At this point, the content of traditional Christian belief may become psychologically problematic because it is associated with a division of the human personality into acceptable and unacceptable aspects, along with a rigorous morality which encourages suppression and repression. Such expectations may inhibit a continuing growth towards psychological maturity and wholeness.

This is all the more the case because there is a certain peril faced by all children as they attempt to establish a sense of individuality for themselves whilst also learning how to relate constructively to other people and to the requirements of social life. Children have to learn how to fit into human society whilst at the same time maintaining their own integrity and perspectives on the world. Many people have been brought up to realise that, although their parents loved them, certain actions on their part would bring about the withdrawal of their acceptance. The revisionist Freudian psychoanalyst Alice Miller has written about the effects of this withdrawal of love in her book *The Drama of Being a Child* (1987). She describes how some children experience their parents' love as being completely conditional on their good behaviour, and how these children feel that their own identities are not acceptable to their parents. Consequently, they hide the apparently 'bad' parts of themselves from parental view, only displaying those aspects of themselves of which their parents will approve. As a result, they lose awareness of their 'bad' characteristics. Because, if they are to have a sense of self-worth, they must only identify with those aspects of themselves that correspond to the values of their parents, they develop what the paediatrician and child psychoanalyst Donald Winnicott, a student of Melanie Klein, called 'a false self'.

The false self is formed by the adaptations that individuals make to meet the expectations that their parents or others place upon them (Winnicott, 1960/1965, p. 140; Winnicott, 1971a, pp. 131–2; Winnicott, 1986). It is 'false' because it requires children to put on an act to hide from view those features of their personalities that would be criticised or suffer opprobrium if they were noticed. However, this is more than a conscious pretence since it becomes an habitual, and largely unconscious, form of adjustment to the demands of caregivers and other authority figures. Winnicott contrasts the false self with 'the true self', which is another way of speaking of the automatic bodily and instinctual responses of a child or an adult to the events of the moment. For our purposes, it is important to note that the true self responds in a spontaneous and unadaptive manner to external stimuli, and a person who is living as a true self feels alive and real, and is able to be creative. In contrast, one who is living as a false self feels empty and lacking in vitality, and lacks imagination.

The true and false selves are expressions of a person's individuality within a social situation. They are the products of the experienced tension in individuals between the environmental pressure to conform to external demands and the internal experience of instinctual reactions and desires arising from human embodment. People who live as true selves retain an ability to express spontaneous reactions and to hold their own beliefs securely despite other people's disagreement. In contrast, those who live as false selves have surrendered their spontaneity, freedom and integrity to the requirements of their parents or other controlling authorities, substituting patterns of behaviour and opinions acceptable to those authorities for their true selves. It should be noted that they have done this unconsciously, which is why in these circumstances it is appropriate to refer to a false self, rather than to a consciously oppressed self or a hypocritical self designed to please. Perhaps, a better description of the false self would be to call it 'the unconsciously over-adapted self'. Another way of describing it is the 'survival self', a term used by Jungian analyst Donald Kalsched (2003, p. 202). In summary, *the false self is the restricted conscious personality which an individual has had to adopt in order to survive the relational context in which she or he has been raised.*

Those persons who live habitually as false selves are unaware of their true selves; in other words, of the full range, both positive and negative, of their spontaneous emotions, sensations, beliefs and other reactions to the phenomenal world. However, these do not cease to exist; instead, they remain blocked and become unconscious. Because the process of psychoanalysis (Freudian or Jungian) appears to bring back into consciousness repressed perceptions, thoughts, effects and reactions which occurred in the past, I believe the existence of a true self which is not identical to the conscious ego is plausible.

The idea that individuals may possess a true or a false self may appear rather outdated in these days of a postmodern awareness of how much an individual's identity is formed through social interaction and the use of language. Many contemporary theorists reject it because it seems to suggest that there is an essential innate core of individual identity that is not totally dependent upon the social context for its existence and development. The understanding of the nature and even the existence of the self is highly contested in contemporary psychology. Personally, I am not convinced that the experience of selfhood can be entirely attributed to social, linguistic or systemic causes. Modern infant research has shown that babies have a sense of separate identity very early in their lives, possibly in the womb (Stern, 1998; Jacobi, 1999). Furthermore, we each inherit a genetic structure which to a large extent determines the development of our physical and, arguably, also our emotional and intellectual capacities, even though these are all modified by environmental factors; and the experience of having a body provides a basis for a sense of individual distinctiveness that continues throughout life. It seems to me entirely reasonable to maintain that each of us has a unique individual identity that is inborn through our genetic inheritance, and significantly determined by our personal experience of embodiment, as well as being moulded by our physical, interpersonal and cultural environments.

The psychoanalytic tradition originates in a biological theory of instincts and drives, and Jungian psychology is founded on the conviction that there are innate psychological structures which are genetically determined, the archetypes, including an archetype of the Self which is responsible for the development of the individual personality (Jung, 1968). The continuing use of these analytic concepts may be reconciled with contemporary perspectives when it is recalled that much in both the Freudian and Jungian traditions is concerned with the relations between the biologically given qualities of individuals and the familial and cultural environments into which they are born and, furthermore, that the development of the true and false selves takes place in the context of social inter- action, especially that between babies and their mothers or mother substitutes.

As a child, and even as an adult, it takes a great deal of emotional energy to preserve a false self and to deny expres- sion to rejected and forgotten facets of your personality, but for many people this is the only way to survive emotionally. The alternative is to remain aware of an intolerable and terri- fying condition: the feeling of being unloved and unlovable. When children with false selves grow into adults, gaining acceptance through conformity continues to dominate their behaviour. Consequently, they are likely to form relationships in which they pay little attention to their own needs while try- ing very hard to fulfil the desires of their colleagues and partners, and to conform excessively to the demands of parental figures, such as teachers, employers and the govern- ment. In addition, in the religious sphere, the manner in which they picture God will be strongly influenced by the images which they have internalised of their own parents. This means that these individuals will very probably experience God as a God who only gives his love to those who behave in the right way and believe the right things, and will believe, whether consciously or unconsciously, that his love is given conditionally, rather than unconditionally.

While some people have been unfortunate enough only to be loved conditionally by their parents or parent-substitutes, fortunately most have been given more or less unconditional love as well. Even so, most of us have had some experience of rejection or conditional love from our parents. Raising a child unavoidably requires a degree of restraint to be imposed by parents, partly for the safety of the child and partly because all children require appropriate guidance and discipline for the development of a well-balanced personality. What matters is the nature of that discipline and the means by which it is en- forced. Most parents resort at times to means which undermine the sense of worth of their children. Many have been told off in such words as: 'You wicked child, how could you do such a thing?' or 'I'll kill you if you do that again.' Furthermore, many parents fail to praise their children sufficiently, often in the mistaken belief that to do so gives a child an inflated sense of themselves.

At school the rules and the punishments inflicted by teachers are likely to have reinforced the sense that some parts of ourselves are praiseworthy, but that others are bad and deserving of censure or, at least, shame. The lesson learned from authority figures, that acceptance is conditional, is usually confirmed by contemporaries: it is important to conform to the norms of a school class or a subgroup of peers, if one is to be accepted in school. For example, despite all the supposed changes in gender expectations in recent years, boys who are no good at sport may be rejected or scorned by both the athletic lads and many of the girls, and many modern children find that they are social outcasts because they are wearing the wrong brand of trainers. Groups of children and adolescents are often extremely intolerant of non-conformity.

Few, therefore, can come to a belief in God without a certain predisposition to fear that God's love is a conditional love. The stronger this is, the more likely an individual is to be influenced by the fear of God's rejection. This may be true even when someone has been converted. Although a convert may genuinely believe that God accepts them unconditionally, if that individual has been subjected to parenting compromised by conditional love, it is very likely that the old pattern of parental relationship will resurface and subtly corrupt the new relationship with both God and the community of believers.

Whatever they may say to the contrary, those Christian traditions which proclaim the reality of heaven and hell in effect only offer the love of God to believers if certain preconditions of belief and behaviour are fulfilled. The normative relationship between God and the adherents of these traditions easily comes to be experienced by them, even if only unconsciously, as equivalent to that between an infant and a mother whose love is experienced as primarily conditional. Hence, this type of Christianity reinforces those neurotic forms of psychological development that tend to accompany child-rearing based on conditional love by encouraging church members to be adaptive in their relationships with both God and their fellow Christians. As a result, rather than bringing freedom, Christian commitment will in all probability result in conformity to external demands for religious compliance. Rather than producing maturity, it will encourage neurotic and immature forms of living.

Spiritual Abuse and the Terrible Choice

A person looking for love and acceptance from God through embracing the Christian religion in practice seeks to receive this love and acceptance from the Christian community and, in particular, from those who hold authority within it, its priests, pastors and teachers. This means that these personnel often have considerable, even excessive, influence over the lives of church members, especially those who are young or lonely or going through a period of vulnerability or transition, such as conversion, divorce or bereavement. Such individuals are at risk of becoming the victims of what has been termed 'spiritual abuse'. This should not be confused with sexual abuse (which will be discussed in Chapter Five), since spiritual abuse usually does not involve any sexual behaviour. However, the manner in which the spiritual abuser undermines the true wishes of his or her victim is similar to the techniques of the sexual abuser, and sometimes spiritual abuse does take the form of sexual abuse.

Spiritual abuse is the subtle, but nevertheless extremely damaging, use of spiritual authority to persuade a person to act in ways which are damaging to her or his individual identity and integrity in the name of obedience to a higher religious purpose. As Johnson and von Voderon explain:

> Spiritual abuse can occur when a leader uses his or her spiritual position to control and dominate another person. It often involves overriding the feelings and opinions of another, without regard to what will result in the other person's state of living, emotions or spiritual well-being. In this application, power is used to bolster the position or needs of a leader, over and above one who comes to them in need. (Johnson and von Vonderon, 1991, pp. 20–1, cited by Wehr, 2000, p. 53)

Although some religious leaders deliberately exploit those under their pastoral care, spiritual abuse may occur even though the abuser has 'the best of intentions' for his or her victim. Religious leaders usually follow the teachings of their Churches and, as a result, may impose conventional spiritual practices on their charges which are oppressive and psychologically destructive because their traditions are themselves oppressive and psychologically destructive. Furthermore, clergy may act abusively because of unconscious needs of their own, including a power drive, or simply because they are psychologically ignorant and are unaware of the damage that they are doing. We will examine such abuses further in Chapter Five.

Spiritual abuse is, I believe, very common in the Church, although it is not widely recognised as such, because often it takes quite covert forms. An awareness of the more extreme examples can open our eyes to the presence of their milder equivalents in the normal pastoral practices of the Church. How it occurs is explained by Jungian analyst Demaris Wehr:

> Most spiritual paths demand that followers set aside 'self', by which they mean selfishness, self-centredness, and the like, and pursue a higher purpose. However, by setting aside self, certain essential attributes may be sacrificed for the greater good. These may include such things as personal goals and desires. There is a very fine line in most spiritual paths, often one that is not sufficiently addressed, between the desirability of being

> self-abnegating for the greater good and being self-
> abnegating in a way that sacrifices one's integrity; in
> other words, that gets one acting in a way that is not in
> accord with one's deepest, truest values. To be healthy,
> one's deepest, truest values must include one's own
> needs. (Wehr, 2000, p. 50)

The 'setting aside of self' is a normal requirement of Christian
spirituality, and there is in all great spiritual traditions much
teaching about self-abnegation which can easily be misunderstood. Such spiritual traditions can be used by religious
leaders to underwrite their own authority, or to impose their
own prescriptions for spiritual flourishing upon such of their
followers who are seeking for personal affirmation through
their faith. In other words, insofar as believers are engaging in
their religion from a position of emotional dependency, they
are vulnerable to exploitation or manipulation by the religious
leader or group in whom they have put their trust. At some
point they are likely to be asked to surrender their own
integrity to the vision of their religious leader or group.
Demaris Wehr describes this surrender as a *'terrible choice'*:

> In all spiritual abuse there comes a time when the
> follower is faced with a 'terrible choice': a choice
> between his or her deepest sense about a situation, intu-
> itions, repressed knowing (which may show up in bodily
> symptoms), and the abuser's view of the situation. While
> other elements of spiritual abuse are specific to particu-
> lar situations, the terrible choice is generic. (Wehr, 2000,
> p. 50)

The terrible choice can be presented in many different
forms. It may come as an invitation to idealise a spiritual
leader and to give over control of one's life to him. It may
come as the insistence by a 'charismatic' group that a member
with a suicidal depression should not seek medical assistance,
but turn to Christ and pray for spiritual healing instead. It
may come as the encouragement of a religious vocation by a

priest, who is more concerned to boost his own sense of having a 'successful' ministry than in discerning what the best future for the young person concerned might be. It may come as the advice given to a battered wife to disregard her own safety and to stay with her husband, in order to fulfil her marriage vows. It may come as the demand that a troubled person should repent, rather than explore the meaning of his psychological disturbance. It may come as guidance in confession or spiritual direction which draws on the moral teaching of the Church in a manner that disregards the empirical reality and practical options open to the penitent. All these, and many other examples, I have encountered in the stories told me by people I have met in my ministry.

The God of Group Belonging

The terrible choice is, however, not confined to individual pastoral relationships; very commonly it is a requirement of church membership. Because membership of a religious group involves to a greater or lesser degree conformity to its boundary conditions, its religious, intellectual and moral norms, the price to a believer of acceptance by a Christian community may be very great. James Alison is a gay Dominican priest who came out and has suffered discrimination and exclusion by the Catholic hierarchy as a result. Although he speaks from a particular type of experience, which some readers may find distasteful or unacceptable, what he has learned about how the Church often deals with non-conformists has a much wider application. The dynamics he describes operate in many different circumstances and, as we shall see, exclude many others than homosexuals from full participation in the Church. Alison's depiction of what being in the Church may be like for gay people is disturbing:

> The experience of many gay people is that the Church in some way or other, kills us ... Typically our inclusion within the structures of church life comes at a very high

price: that of agreeing not to speak honestly, of disguising our experience with a series of euphemisms, of having to maintain, through a coded language shared with other 'insiders' within the system, a double life. The message is: you're fine just so long as you don't rock the boat through talking frankly, which is the same as saying: 'You're protected while you play the game our way, but the moment that something "comes to light", you're out. The moment you say something which causes scandal, watch out!' (Alison, 2001, p. 45)

In many religious contexts gay people find that their continuance in the Church is conditional on adherence to traditional Christian teaching forbidding the genital expression of same-sex love. Many Christians would think that such a restriction is right and proper, since they regard homosexual and lesbian sexual activity as sinful. Others disagree. But whatever your position is, it should be clear that it is extremely costly for a gay person to belong to the Church on condition that he restrains from all same-sex sexual intimacy. For such a one, belonging to the Church may well be experienced as entailing the sacrifice of an essential aspect of his identity, especially when abstinence is associated with a silence about his sexuality that amounts to hypocrisy. Numerous gay men and women have found it impossible to conform to this requirement, and may feel that the Church acts abusively towards them.

To hide aspects of one's nature in order to gain and retain membership of a church is destructive of a person's individuality and integrity. Even more damaging to such an individual is to internalise the values of the group to which he wishes to belong and to apply that group's condemnation of those hidden aspects of his character internally to himself. Alison describes what this is like for the gay person:

At root, I myself believed that God was on the side of ecclesiastical violence directed at gay people, and couldn't believe that God loves us just as we are. The profound 'do not *be*' which the social and ecclesiastical voice speaks to us, and which forms the soul of so many gay people, was profoundly rooted in my own being, so that, *au fond*, I felt myself damned. (Alison, 2001, p. 39)

A religious affiliation of this nature can hardly be liberating; can hardly be good news. The gay experience makes the demand so often presented by the Christian religion to its adherents very clear: *in some aspect of your self you must not be.* For a gay man, this includes both the genital expression of same-sex love and also the positive evaluation of homoerotic feelings. The message of this 'gospel' is that if both are rejected, then and only then may acceptance be gained from both God and the Church.

Churchgoers may sacrifice some element of their fundamental identity or need in order to gain acceptance within their Christian communities. The nature and consequences of the choice to make such a sacrifice are illuminated by Alison's conception of *the god of group belonging.* Alison explains the nature of the sacrifice this 'god' requires in order to confer group belonging:

First there is a logic in which 'god' and 'being' are linked to the social group and to belonging. This is the logic which says to us: 'We can allow you to belong, in fact we can give you real being which comes from our god, if you go along with us in annihilating the part of your being which is over-against our group belonging. What you think is part of your being is not really any such thing, it is an evil spirit, or a spiritual sickness which can be cured, or at least neutralised. Allow us to treat it as such, and you can be part of us'. . . And many of us have gone along with this, for how long, and at what cost! (Alison, 2001, pp. 128–9)

Those who are emotionally immature or vulnerable are particularly liable to surrender themselves to the god of group belonging. As we have seen, those Christians whose belief that God loves them is tempered by a fear, conscious or unconscious, that he will reject them very frequently fall victim to a deep-seated anxiety. Such fear arises from their individual need to feel accepted by God, but becomes all the more pressing when their membership of a social group and, thus, their social identity is tied to conformity to a group belief. The threat of exclusion or marginalisation is often implicit within the culture of a church or Christian group concerned to maintain its 'purity'. In such cases, the gospel, instead of bringing new life and freedom, tends to restrict the lives of its adherents. They are likely to adopt behaviour acceptable to their congregations and to accept the definitions of truth promoted by them in a rather uncritical or even rigid manner.

Even those who are not noticeably emotionally insecure or immature may learn to hide their true opinions. The President of Ireland, Mary McAleese, is a good example of one who adopted this strategy. She describes how the combination of clerical authority and the habit of deference led her, as a Roman Catholic in Northern Ireland when a young woman, to avoid stating openly her support for the ordination of women to the priesthood:

> To challenge the awesome authority of the hierarchy seemed to open an aptly named Pandora's box of things which might be difficult to swallow. If the Church was wrong, on an issue on which it spoke with a chilling clarity and certainty, then how many other errors might lie buried in that theology. There was a comfort in burying myself inside the group consciousness and putting my hands over my ears so that I could not hear the doubts that were running about in my head. To pit myself against the group meant challenging mother, father, family, parish, community and to live with some form of exclusion which, whether mild rebuke or subtle shunning, would inevitably follow. (McAleese, 1997, p. 41)

In other words, she knew that if she challenged the god of

group belonging, she would be punished in some way. She concludes, 'it was easier to feign ignorance than to face doubt' (McAleese, 1997, p. 42).

Institutional Spiritual Abuse and Internalised Oppression

Spiritual abuse may take place at an institutional level, not just at an individual one, and may be explicitly associated with the demand to surrender to the god of group belonging. For example, whilst I was writing this section, I opened the *Irish Times* and read the headline 'Vatican accused of "spiritual abuse" of women'. Underneath was a story about the opening of the first Women's Ordination Worldwide Conference, an unofficial Roman Catholic gathering, in Dublin:

> Nobel prize winner Ms Mairead Corrigan Maguire has said that the Vatican's stance on the ordination of women is 'dehumanising, demoralising, and is a form of spiritual abuse' . . . And this 'spiritual violence is experienced not only by women, but also by theologians, priests, religious and laity. We are all aware of the Vatican's practice of "silencing" those whose opinions differ.
>
> 'In a time when dialogue is being called for by both secular, state, and church bodies, Irish society is permeated with fear amongst clergy and religious, of speaking out on issues such as women's ordination. Indeed they have tragically been forbidden to do so,' she said. (*Irish Times*, Saturday 30 June 2001, p. 5)

In many churches women are now ordained, but not in the Roman Catholic Church. In the encyclical *Ordinatio Sacerdotalis*, the Pope restated the traditional Catholic arguments against the ordination of women, and required theologians to stop debating the matter. Sister Lavinia Byrne, who was at the time in the process of publishing a book, *Women at the Altar*, which questioned the papal prohibition of women's ordination, despite having obtained the necessary canonical permissions to publish, discovered that her publisher in the United States of America was reneging on the agreement to publish the book. After a long and painful period, during which pressure was put upon her order and herself to adhere to the party line, and to refrain from making any public statements about the matter, she decided to leave the religious community to which she belonged. She explains:

> I was asking to leave the community because I could no longer bear to be part of an institution which had, of necessity, to uphold bits of Catholic teaching which were being used to persecute me and my conscience and the consciences of thousands of women who thought like me. Better to be out and sane than to remain in and go mad with the compromise of silence that was forced upon me. (Byrne, 2000, p. 190)

The examples of gay people and of the ordination of women within the Roman Catholic Church are both controversial and obvious cases where membership of, and acceptance within, a Christian community requires conformity to particular restraints which are experienced by some individuals as subversive of their integrity. However, the existence and destructive effects of submission to the god of group belonging within the Church are normally much less obvious than in the case of the silencing and restraint of gay Christians and women who want to be ordained. It is very common for those who wish to belong to a church to be expected to adhere, at least to a significant degree, to the normative social mores of that congregation, including its ideological outlook and the intellectual restrictions of its system of belief. Belonging to the group provides strong emotional benefits, but it may be bought at a considerable psychological cost to the individuals concerned, and this may amount to what is known as 'internalised oppression'.

Internalised oppression is the process by which subordinate groups internalise and identify with the values of their oppressors and thus devalue or deny the legitimacy or truth of their own alternative perceptions based on their own knowledge and experience. The ideological identification of the values and interests of a social group with the will of God is a powerful source of reassurance and justification for those who belong to such groups and regard themselves as especially favoured by God. Paradoxically, it can give affirmation not only to those who are privileged but also to those who are lower down the social order, and who suffer deprivation or oppression from the economic and political arrangements in that society. They can find a sense of virtue and acceptance from God through accepting the teaching that these social structures are willed by him. So long as they are obedient, humbly accepting the position in life given them by God, they feel assured that he loves and approves of them. As a consequence, many Christians conform to social structures supported by an oppressive ideology.

History is full of examples of subordinate social classes being offered salvation from God and a place in the Church on condition that they accept that their subordination is willed by God. This includes those who were economically inferior, such as women, slaves, servants and colonised races. The Christian religion has often acted as an ideology supporting this inequality, and individuals have only been fully incorporated into the Christian community on condition that they surrender fundamental aspects of their identity and self-determination to these group norms. In such circumstances individuals identify internally with the teachings of the ideology and seek to live in accordance with them, even though this may mean that they voluntarily restrict their freedom and self-determination. The outer circumstances of exclusion and subordination are not simply enforced by the external authorities; they become part of the belief system of the one who is disadvantaged by them. Individuals are presented with a pattern of living that is said to have been willed by God, to which they are expected to adhere because of their membership of a particular social group, and they internalise uncritically its belief system as their own. As a result, they experience God's acceptance of themselves as conditional upon their own acceptance of a subordinate social status.

Ironically, such group norms also restrict the lives of members of the dominant class, because they too have an ideal of behaviour which they are expected to meet. For instance, men are expected to be tough and to repress their vulnerability and, in the Church, ordained ministers are expected to act in a Christ-like manner. Both the dominant and subordinate groups in a Christian society, which is identified with an ideology, are forced to disown those aspects of their characters which do not fit the role allocated to them by that ideology. Only if they do this are they able to find full acceptance in that society and Church, and thus to receive the assurance that they are also loved and accepted by God. Since the acceptance of God is held by them to be conditional on such personal renunciation, the Gospel of Conditional Love provides a strong motivation for the acceptance of unjust social arrangements by believers, and for the self-restraint and social conformity of both privileged and disadvantaged social classes.

CHAPTER FOUR

Integrating the Christian Shadow

The Shadow and its Projection

The cost of belonging to the Church is very great when it involves Christians in sacrificing essential aspects of their personalities and restricting their thinking to the 'orthodoxies' of their ecclesiastical communities. As has been already mentioned, this may entail any or all of the following: the adoption of an over-restrictive persona; living as a false self; making the terrible choice; conforming to the god of group belonging; and internalised oppression. In addition, believers may be the objects of spiritual abuse either from an individual pastor or from the church organisation itself. Given the fact that so many of the devout are prepared to accept these detrimental effects of membership, the emotional benefits of being a part of the Church must be experienced as extremely valuable by them. These advantages appear to be found primarily in the security and certainty that being a member of a religious group may confer. It is tragic that so many believers are prepared to put up with these conditions of membership in order to gain these benefits, and it is not at all surprising that the churches have experienced a continuous haemorrhage from their membership over the past century and more of those who are not prepared to limit themselves in these ways.

However, those aspects of themselves to which church-goers deny expression do not cease to exist but covertly cause many problems. These may be illuminated by Jung's concept of 'the shadow'. In circumstances where some aspects of their personalities, beliefs or behaviour are unacceptable to themselves or others, whether parents, lovers, contemporaries, authority figures, fellow churchgoers or God, individual Christians may split off and repress those features. Such split-off or repressed aspects of a person, of which the ego remains largely unaware, Jung called the shadow. *The individual or personal shadow* 'is made up essentially of contents which have at one time been conscious but which have disappeared from consciousness through having been forgotten or repressed' (Jung, 1936/1937/1968, p. 42, para. 88). It is roughly equivalent to Freud's idea of the subconscious personality. It should be distinguished from *the collective or archetypal shadow* which, according to Jung, represents those dark aspects of human nature, including evil itself, which are characteristic of the human race as a whole and have their origin in the collective depths of the unconscious, not in the personal history of the individual (Jung, 1957/1970, pp. 296–7, para. 572). This latter is an idea which is not shared by the Freudian tradition of psychology.

It is important to note that although the personal shadow is made up of aspects of the personality which remain hidden from the light of consciousness, and which individuals are unable to acknowledge as part of themselves, its contents are not necessarily negative; part of them may consist of characteristics which are potentially creative but which have not been developed. For example, self-assertion may have been crushed by an upbringing which treated any assertion of will as selfishness. Individuals who have experienced such an education may behave in an overly passive or obedient manner, both to figures of authority and more generally, but have a shadow which contains a drive towards self-assertion that would be extremely helpful in enabling them to stand up for themselves and their legitimate rights at work, or in their family. Whether it is made up of positive or negative features, the shadow contains whatever an individual cannot accept about him- or herself. As Jung says: 'The shadow personifies everything that the subject refuses to acknowledge about himself and yet is always thrusting itself upon him directly or indirectly – for instance, inferior traits of character and other incompatible tendencies' (Jung, 1939/1968, pp. 284–5, para. 513).

Although Christians may identify themselves with the righteousness promoted by the god of group belonging and serve the Church in a conscious attempt to serve God, their shadows continue to exist unconsciously. Indeed, the cost of the ego's identification with 'virtue' is the relegation to the shadow of all incompatible tendencies, because the identification can only be sustained if everything that might contradict it is cut off from conscious awareness. According to Jung: 'We do not like to look at the shadowside of ourselves; therefore there are many people in our civilized society who have lost their shadow altogether, they have got rid of it. They are only two-dimensional; they have lost the third dimension, and with it they have usually lost the body' (Jung, 1935/1977, p. 23, para. 40). Even if they do not cause neuroses, repressed aspects of Christians' personalities continue to influence their actions, and may become the source of some of the most unattractive features of the behaviour of Christians, because what is repressed does not cease to exist (Jung, 1938/1969, p. 76, para. 131), and the more difficult it is to accept the more a person has to fight him- or herself in order to keep it unconscious. As David Freeman, a rabbi and Jungian analyst, explains:

> The greater the denial which we carry inside ourselves – the bigger lies we go on and on telling ourselves – then the more we have to be afraid of and avoid the truth. To guard ourselves from harm, we have to establish an inner tyranny in order to censor it away. For instance, if a person lives a life of pretence, denying what he knows

to be true, pushing away truths because he is afraid to look at them, he will have to be utterly dictatorial with himself. He will require his own inner equipment, bullies and secret police force to protect his deceptions and allow through only what will not change anything. He will victimise any parts of himself striving to be free, parts of him that are Scharansky or Mandela. We all have these parts, bits inside us which rise up from time to time and try to challenge the lies. He, like all totalitarian regimes, will persuade himself that he is strong, but really he is so weak that he needs vast armies to enforce his will and to protect him. (Freeman, 1991, p. 4)

Those aspects of the personality that are denied and repressed by the conscious mind continue to be active in an individual's unconscious mental world, and are likely to be projected. In other words, they continue to be experienced by the ego, but as if they belonged to other people. *Projection* is one of the defence mechanisms associated with splitting or, as Jung preferred to call it, dissociation. Particular persons or groups become *identified* in a projector's mind with those features of her or his own personality that have become split off from consciousness. It is important to note that, as in the case of repression, projection is an unconscious process; the individual does not recognise what she or he is doing. The result is that those others who have become identified or merged in a person's mind with unconscious contents are perceived *as if* they actually had those unacknowledged traits (von Franz, 1980).

For example, a man who has denied and repressed his own anger and aggression may experience other people as being aggressive towards him, although they are not intending to act in an aggressive manner. He may perceive any slight brusqueness or tardiness in responding to him as a put-down, and may at the same time act in a critical and inconsiderate manner towards them. Indeed, it is very probable that his own behaviour will incite them to attack him in retaliation, thereby justifying his sense that others are always hostile to him, and blinding him to the fact that it was his own aggressiveness that provoked the conflict in the first place.

Those who repress unacceptable parts of themselves project them onto suitable victims and experience their own doubts, fears, anger, etc., *as if they belonged to those others*. This enables the projectors to maintain a sense of their own moral virtue and mental stability. Furthermore, *those who carry such projections will be treated by the projectors in a manner equivalent to their internal treatment of those repressed and projected elements*. Thus, for example, if someone is very harsh with his own sexuality, he will be equally condemning of anyone else who acts out his repressed sexual desires or, for whatever reason, is perceived by him as being sexually provocative. Likewise, if a Christian believer cannot face her own doubts, she is very likely to criticise any who voice such doubts and attempt to silence them. However, unlike these cases, there need be no reality supporting such projections. A projection may take place on the basis of physical characteristics or of some other factor that is not directly related to the quality that is projected, such as a difference in belief. This is very commonly the case in situations of persecution or religious conflict in which the victims of the persecution receive all sorts of negative projections which their behaviour does not merit. One only has to look at Christian anti-Semitism, or the mutual anathemas of Protestants and Catholics, to recognise the unmerited nature and destructive consequences of such projections.

Scapegoating in the Church

Christians may also project their negative characteristics onto other people who, consequently, come to represent unacceptable parts of themselves and may be blamed for the stirring of unwelcome desires. For example, in much traditional Christian teaching about women, they are portrayed as temptresses made in the image of Eve and portrayed as the original source of man's (i.e. the male's) downfall. In consequence, over the centuries women have often been blamed for the fact that most men feel compelling sexual desire for them. Such blaming may amount to what is known as 'scapegoating', which is another unconscious means very commonly used by Christians to protect a sense of their own righteousness, and one which results in many destructive disturbances in the relationships between individuals and groups.

Scapegoating is a term that originates in a rite performed on the Jewish Day of Atonement, the description of which is found in Leviticus, chapter 16. In this ceremony the high priest confessed the sins of the sons of Israel over the head of the scapegoat, which was then sent into the wilderness carrying them with it, thereby purifying the community of those sins. This ceremony was a conscious means by which the Hebrews acknowledged their faults and were cleansed from them. It was a psychologically healthy ritual to the extent that it necessitated the Hebrews becoming aware of, and confessing publicly, the sinful things that they had done. Even so, rather than living with a continuing awareness of their faults, their sinfulness was pushed out of the community into the desert.

The modern psychological form of scapegoating is, in contrast, unconscious and psychologically destructive, because it is the means by which individuals or groups blame other individuals or groups for faults which belong to themselves, but which remain unacknowledged (Perera, 1986, pp. 16–17). This can be done by the exclusion of the goat from the 'righteous' community (as in the ancient Jewish ceremony) or by the elimination of the goat. The projection of shadow qualities is responsible for scapegoating and gives rise to some very unpleasant human behaviour, including religious persecution. When such projection is mutual it results in many conflicts between different social, political and religious groups (von Franz, 1980, pp. 18–19; Neumann, 1973, esp. pp. 33–58; Moses, 1989).

Scapegoat psychology is endemic within the Church. When they identify themselves or their communities with the favour of God, Christians often repress and project those shadowy aspects of their characters that do not conform to the will of God onto scapegoats, who are then blamed and persecuted for having those characteristics. Opposing groups within the Church frequently appear to be projecting their own unconscious negative qualities onto each other. Such projections often fall upon members of the wider Church who hold different doctrinal opinions, or who do not appear to live up to the same ethical standards as those the projectors promote, for example, theological liberals, theological conservatives, Evangelicals, divorcees, homosexuals, and women who believe that they are called to be ordained as priests. This process usually involves qualities which both sides possess but are hidden in their shadows, such as doubt, intolerance or irrationality, and which, through projection, they both experience as belonging to the other. Consequently, it is the 'others' who are experienced as being the ones who are wrong and prejudiced, and who need to change their views and behaviour.

The projection of the negative onto an opposition group enables the projectors to blame that group for the existence of those negative qualities in the Church, thereby avoiding any acknowledgement of their own responsibility and shadow, and maintaining a good conscience. Scapegoating is very often involved in the quest for purity in the Church and is particularly evident in the dispute between liberals and conservatives. This has been evident in the long-standing conflict between those who favour and those who oppose the ordination of women to the priesthood and episcopacy in the Anglican Communion. For example, in a letter to the *Church Times* one advocate for the ordination of women, referring to a group called the Movement for the Continuing Church of England, said:

> The vast majority of loyal Anglicans should pray that such misogynist fanatics be encouraged to move out of parish life as quickly as possible, taking their prejudices and inadequacies with them.

Allegedly the action group (a phrase reminiscent of pre-war Fascism) contains several lay readers. Such people should lose their licences and be denied the opportunity to spread their hate-filled propaganda. (Walker, 1989)

Furthermore, the practice of church discipline has often amounted to scapegoating. The demand by the Reverend Tony Higton for the disciplining of errant clergy which was described in Chapter Two is a good example. He wanted the Church's leadership to restate the doctrine and ethical teaching of the Church in the narrowest of traditional terms, to discipline those whose behaviour or teaching breaks the old rules, and to silence those whose opinions question the old teaching. What Higton's approach amounted to was an ultimatum to the clergy to conform to his criteria or get out. In other words, *the purity of the Church was to be achieved by the exclusion of those singled out as sinners.*

Often particular groups within a Christian community have been identified as sources of disruption or 'evil'. A very good example of this is the numerous young women in Ireland who were confined in the Magdalene laundries run by the Sisters of Mercy, the last of which only closed in 1996. These women were signed into the laundries by their families in the same way that the mentally ill used to be signed into asylums:

> Magdalene girls were cast aside by their families and by society. Their 'sins' varied from being unmarried mothers to being too pretty, simple minded, too clever or a victim of rape and talking about it.
>
> To atone for their 'sins', these girls slaved 364 days a year for no pay. They were half starved, humiliated and often beaten. About 40 per cent gave birth outside of wedlock and had had their babies forcibly removed from them. Their sentence was indefinite and thousands lived and died in these harsh loveless places. (Donohoe, 2002)

They were scapegoats for the dangers of female sexuality in respectable Irish Catholic society, and were removed from the general population because they had either offended against the 'purity' required of women or were deemed to be at risk of provoking men's sexual desire or, sometimes, simply because there was nowhere else for them to go. They are a recent example of the ancient Christian tendency to blame women for both the arousal of male sexual desire, and men's sexual misbehaviour.

Across the centuries, scapegoating has been commonly observed both in the internal relations of Christian denominations and between them, as in the conflict between Catholics and Protestants. However, the scapegoating of others by Christians need not be confined to those within the Christian fold. In Christian history it has been common for whole groups of 'deviant' others to be scapegoated. Heretics and non-Christians have been the objects of scapegoating, giving rise to Wars of Religion between Christians, or against Moslems, and the forcible conversion or enslavement of pagans. Such groups have received the projection of Christians' unconscious disbelief or resistance to God, and then been punished for it. Likewise, in Europe women have been scapegoated and burnt or hanged as witches in order to assuage Christian men's fear of women, the body and nature, all of which have at times been demonised by Christian tradition. The most notorious victims of the Christian practice of scapegoating have been the Jews, who have frequently been reviled for 'killing Christ' (a Jew himself) and have been the victims of restrictive laws, persecutions and pogroms, culminating in the Holocaust. In Nazi Germany the Jews were blamed for all the ills of the German people and six million of them were exterminated, along with the mentally ill and handicapped, homosexuals, gypsies and other 'undesirables' in order to 'cleanse' the German nation.

Erich Neumann, a Jew and one of Jung's closest associates, shortly after the Second World War wrote a book, *Depth Psychology and a New Ethic* (1973), seeking to explain how it was that Western civilisation had given birth to two world wars and the Holocaust. He laid the blame at the door of what he called 'the Old Ethic', that is to say, the ethical teaching which requires its adherents to live up to a high ideal and, in so doing, to suppress or repress their shadow side. In order for those practising the Old Ethic to remain unaware of their shadows, Neumann claimed, it was necessary for them to project their shadows onto others who could be blamed and attacked. In other words, it was necessary for them to engage in scapegoat psychology. His hypothesis provides an explanation for how it is that Christians, who preach a gospel of God's unconditional love, are able, despite the clear contradiction, to torture, execute and go to war with their fellow human beings in the name of that God. *When the exclusionary processes entailed by the Christian complex are combined with the ideological assimilation of Christianity to a particular political programme and the identification of a particular nation with God's chosen people, the potential for ideological closure, intolerance, the persecution of opponents and war to result is very great indeed.*

A Summary of the Effects of the Christian Complex

We are now in a position to summarise the structure and dynamics of the Christian complex. Importantly, it is not confined to individual psychology, but gives rise to a series of interconnected behaviours and attitudes at the social as well as the individual level. The figure overleaf shows the Christian complex in diagrammatic form. Note how it is made up of a pattern of relations which are circular or recursive and which, consequently, reinforces itself. The diagram shows the complex's systemic structure very well.

The emotional core of the Christian complex is the combination within individuals of the desire to be loved with the fear of rejection. Individuals may use the Christian religion in two related ways to meet their need for love and acceptance. The first is by seeking love directly from God, whether in the form of the Father or Jesus or the Holy Spirit, or indirectly

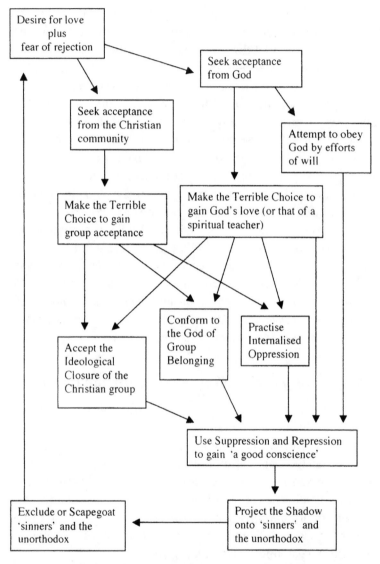

The Christian complex in diagrammatic form

from his heavenly representatives, Mary and the saints; and the second is by looking for love from the Christian community. Of course, it is possible to have a relationship with either God or the Christian community which does not involve the

Christian complex. However, although individuals may discover the acceptance of God through an adherence to Christianity, they are also very likely to be influenced, consciously or unconsciously, by the awareness that, according to the Bible and much church teaching, God's love is in many respects conditional on their behaviour or belief. In many people the complex develops because their fear of rejection leads them in one way or another to make the terrible choice in order to gain God's approval or that of the Christian community. This means that in some way they give up an aspect of their identity that is essential to their integrity, maybe becoming the two-dimensional people mentioned earlier. They conform to an ideal of Christian virtue or the commands of a spiritual leader or the respectable mores of the Christian group that are unduly restrictive of their personalities and injurious to their psychological well-being. Forms of the terrible choice that I have identified may be grouped together under the following headings:

(a) conformity to the teaching of a spiritual guide;
(b) conformity to the god of group belonging;
(c) conformity to the ideological closure of the Christian group;
(d) internalised oppression.

Those aspects of such Christians' characters or thoughts that are not consistent with the requirements of Christian virtue and belief, or the social mores and ideological commitments of their own Christian groups (the demands of the god of group belonging), are relegated to the shadow. Since they do not cease to exist, these are projected onto other people who do not belong to the same community or share the same beliefs, or who break the behavioural expectations of the group. Such people are either excluded or penalised in some way by the group, acting as scapegoats for those aspects of itself which it cannot accept because it believes that God does not accept them.

The practices of scapegoating, exclusion and blaming that

are apparent within the Christian community, however they are manifested, are observed by its members. They recognise, at least unconsciously, that the Church does not truly practise a gospel of unconditional acceptance, and that the love of God mediated by the Christian community has conditions attached to it. Their fears of rejection by God and the Church are, thereby, reinforced and they are all the more careful to fulfil the conditions of acceptance laid down by Christian teaching and the god of group belonging so that they too do not experience its condemnation. They seek to live up to the demands of the Christian persona either through deliberate efforts of will or unconsciously through projection and scapegoating, and may well develop a false self adapted to Christian expectations, or they may resort to hypocrisy so that, at least, they appear to be virtuous.

The Christian complex does not always have severe consequences, but there is an organic connection between the core emotional need to find acceptance from God, the fear of rejection and the psychological dynamics of splitting and projection which, ultimately, give rise to scapegoating, and, because of this, the complex is a frequent feature of the modes of relationship practised within the Church as well as of the internal lives of individual believers. From a systemic standpoint, the network of interconnected behaviours, beliefs and emotions that constitutes the complex operates both within and between individuals. Indeed, children and converts are inducted into it through the external practices of the Church and its members, through which they learn to internalise the behaviours, beliefs and emotions connected with it. In Jungian terms, the complex exists in the cultural unconscious and is passed on to individuals through the interaction of a person's emotional needs with Christian education and socialisation. Consequently, because churches are normatively assimilated to the cultural context in which they are placed, the conditions for acceptance included in individuals' versions of the complex generally incorporate many aspects of the social mores and ideologies of the cultures and societies to which church members belong.

Jung points out that as well as recognising the fact that we have complexes it is important to know 'that complexes can have us' (Jung, 1948/1969, p. 96, para. 200). In other words, an individual's behaviour and emotions may come to be significantly determined by the contents of a complex, but without the person concerned being aware of this fact. This is manifestly the case with the Christian complex, and this applies not just to individuals but to the institutions of the Christian religion. The cause of many of the evils associated with Christianity may be identified as the combination in the Christian complex of psychological repression and projection with the Gospel of Conditional Love, especially when this takes place in association with ideological closure and the sanctions that maintain group conformity and respectability. Regrettably, there is an organic connection between the need to find acceptance from God, the fear of rejection and the psychological dynamics of splitting and projection which, ultimately, give rise to scapegoating. Christians may use their religion as a way to boost their own egos through identifying themselves and their communities with the righteousness and favour of God, or as a support for their social structures and a justification for their privileges. But, if the God whom they worship is the God of conditional love, all these benefits are bought at a very high psychological cost: they are likely to edit their personalities, which become lop-sided, and to repress their shadows in order to win acceptance from God and other Christians.

The claim that Jesus came to give us life abundantly (John 10:10) is one part of the Christian religion that is open to empirical verification. If the genuine attempt to live a Christian life may result in constriction, neurosis, internalised oppression, ideological closure, scapegoating and, ultimately, war and genocide, the claim is either false or there must be something radically mistaken in the way in which the Christian religion is conceived and practised. I believe it is the latter.

The Christian complex is as dangerous as it is ubiquitous and it is vital for the Church as an institution, and Christians in general, to become aware of it so that they can begin the very painful and difficult task of seeking to heal it. We will now investigate what needs to happen for the Christian religion to be reformed in such a way that it no longer gives birth to the Christian complex and all its terrible consequences.

The Integration of the Shadow and the Healing of the Christian Complex

In principle, any healthy religion should reinforce its adherents' integrity, rather than subverting it by encouraging adaptive behaviour that amounts to dishonesty or hypocrisy and encourages repression. It is, in fact, an ancient teaching of the Christian Church that our true identity is hid with God, and that following Christ is the way in which a person may most authentically discover his or her true self; and, conversely, that the way to come to know God is through knowing yourself. Fundamentally, Christian spirituality is about the connection of everything to God who is present in all things. Much traditional Christian spirituality is concerned with enabling worshippers to discover God as the centre of their lives.

Nevertheless, this cannot happen unless the devout are also prepared to recognise the full range, both positive and negative, of their personalities. At the core of any genuine Christian spirituality (as also of psychological growth from a Jungian or Winnicottian perspective) is the transformation of individuals into their authentic or true selves, and this cannot be achieved either by efforts of will or by psychological splitting. Jung criticised Christianity for being a religion that promotes perfection at the cost of wholeness. I agree with Jung that the religion of perfection, in other words, Pharisaism and the Gospel of Conditional Love, is a perversion of what Christianity should be. Only a recognition that the mission of Jesus was to destroy the religion of perfection and the psychological division associated with it will be able to make the Christian religion into a vehicle for psychological wholeness.

Neumann is helpful in this regard; he argued for a change from an ethic of perfection to one of consciousness. In other words, he said that it was necessary for individuals to take responsibility not only for their conscious actions, but also for their unconscious ones; they could not hold themselves innocent merely because they had been unconscious of what they did or of the consequences of their actions (Neumann, 1973). Following Neumann, I believe that *Christians must take responsibility for the repercussions of the psychological split that lies at the core of orthodox doctrine and for its innumerable destructive effects.* It is no good saying that Christianity is about the unconditional love of God, and that it can enable believers to grow in imitation of Christ's selfless and sacrificial love, if the attempt to follow Christ often results, however unintentionally, in the evils which I have described. For Jung and Neumann the solution to this paradox of Christian practice is to recognise that the first stage in the development of human wholeness is to face and integrate its shadow side. This is a stage in emotional growth that cannot be by-passed without incurring the severe consequences that I have indicated. Hence, this is where the healing of the Christian complex must begin.

The withdrawal of projections is an essential feature of the integration of the shadow; it is also an important means of growing in both psychological and spiritual maturity, because projectors have not only to recognise that the projections have taken place, and that the 'projectiles' are in fact unacknowledged parts of themselves, but also to come to a new relationship with those aspects of their characters (von Franz, 1980, p. 10). This is where the chief difficulty lies; it is extremely painful and humiliating for anybody to acknowledge inferior or less developed traits; and it is very demanding, since they may require development or education. For instance, the man with an authoritarian character, described in the last chapter, would need not only to recognise that he himself acted in an authoritarian way, but also to adapt his behaviour towards his inferiors and his attitude towards his superiors, as well as facing his own unconscious sense of inferiority. All this is very consuming of time and energy, and is often achieved only after considerable struggle, possibly requiring psychotherapeutic help. And yet as Jung writes: 'Suffering that is not understood is hard to bear, while on the other hand it is often astounding to see how much a person can endure when he understands the why and the wherefore' (Jung, 1956/1977, p. 698, para. 1578).

Also, there is a further difficulty described by Marie Louise von Franz, one of Jung's closest collaborators:

> unconscious contents can scarcely ever be integrated into the subject in their entirety . . . Consequently a phenomenon occurs that could be described as *the wandering of projections*: the unconscious content is in part recognised as subjective and thereby differentiated from the object in which it hitherto appeared as a projection; its still-unrecognised aspect, however, appears again projected into another medium, which now becomes the bearer of the projection. (von Franz, 1980, p. 13, italics in original)

Thus, for example, a man who falls in love with a woman may project onto her many qualities which she does not possess. When he discovers this, his projections will be dissolved and withdrawn. Some may be integrated, but those which are not will lie latent until such time as another woman attracts them and the cycle begins again.

Many Christians find the idea of integrating the shadow very disturbing. It sounds as if they are being asked to live out all their most unattractive and sinful desires. However, this is not what is meant. *The essential feature of this process is not behaviour but awareness*; the point is to learn to live with as full an awareness as possible of all aspects of one's character, whether commendable or not, without resorting to repression and its entailments, projection and scapegoating, in order to avoid the vision of one's own weakness, foolishness, selfishness and outright evil or, perplexingly, of one's unlived strength, wisdom, love and virtue. Paradoxically, to integrate the shadow requires each of us to learn to love and accept ourselves as we really are without making excuses or blaming others for our refusal to use all of our God-given talents. It is actually a very difficult and humbling form of psychological growth and has much in common with traditional forms of self-examination in Christian spirituality.

The integration of the shadow is also necessary if we are genuinely to be able to love either God or our neighbour and, as such, is not only consistent with Jesus' great commandment that we should love God and our neighbour as ourselves (Mark 12:30–1; Matthew 22:37–9), but is implicitly required by it. In order to obey Christ's command to love our neighbours as ourselves, it is first necessary to love ourselves. Conversely, to allow ourselves to be loved necessitates us learning to love ourselves. If we do not, we will simply project what we cannot accept about ourselves onto our neighbours and reject them as we try to make ourselves 'good enough for God'. In addition, we may push God away on the grounds that we are not worthy of his love. In brief, if we are to obey Christ, we need to stop fighting against the unacceptable sides of our characters and seek to come to terms with them. However, none of us likes to face the fact that much of what we do is nothing like as virtuous or praiseworthy as we pretend to ourselves and to others that it is. Assimilating the shadow is an extremely tricky and costly procedure which takes time and considerable courage, and yet unless we do so we cannot develop a mature attitude to others or ourselves; we remain very one-sided.

Unconditional Love and the Integration of the Shadow in Psychotherapy

This process may be encouraged by the positive, affirming and caring attitude of a psychoanalyst or psychotherapist. The practice of psychotherapy shows that deep inner healing can be facilitated through a love that wills the best for a person whilst knowing the worst. An experience of unconditional love may enable individuals to accept the reality of the people they happen to be because it makes it unnecessary to reject or repress the less desirable aspects of their characters. Paradoxically, such acceptance does not encourage individuals to become immoral or self-centred; rather, it is the essential foundation for the development of a genuine concern for others. This is because when individuals have had their needs for love and acceptance met, they are freed from the compulsion to seek for their satisfaction through other people or through religion. It becomes possible for them to stop splitting their personalities into two, as Alice Miller has witnessed in her psychoanalytic practice:

> Splitting of the human being into two parts, one that is good, meek, conforming, and obedient and the other that is the diametrical opposite is perhaps as old as the human race, and one could simply say that it is part of 'human nature'. Yet it has been my experience that when people have had the opportunity to seek and live out their true self in analysis, this split disappears of itself. They perceive both sides, the conforming as well as the so-called obscene, as two extremes of the false self, which they now no longer need. (Miller, 1985, pp. 192–3)

In addition, one who learns that she is accepted 'warts and all' by another person is able to remain conscious and accepting of her own warts, and not see them on the faces of those in her environment.

People who discover their true selves are those who are in direct touch with their own feelings. They are not repressed. Thus, they are able to react spontaneously and they feel alive in a way that those who have split-off aspects of themselves rarely do. Such people have no serious temptation to surrender their souls to the Christian group, because they already have the sense of their own value which others are looking for through group membership. As Miller explains:

those who have spontaneous feelings can only be themselves. They have no other choice if they want to remain true to themselves. Rejection, ostracism, loss of love, and name calling will not fail to affect them; they will suffer as a result and will dread them, but once they have found their authentic self they will not want to lose it. And when they sense something is being demanded of them to which their whole being says no, they cannot do it. They simply cannot. (Miller, 1983, p. 85)

At its best psychotherapy enables individuals to have an experience of acceptance through the relationship with the therapist and, to a degree, to be freed from psychological splitting and repression and from having to maintain a false self. In this way psychotherapy may bring about emotional healing and an increase in personal freedom.

The implication for Christianity is that, if it is to be a truly healing form of belief, the love of God must be seen to be analogous to that of the therapeutic attitude of unconditional acceptance provided by the psychotherapist. For me, this does not mean an indifference to those aspects of people's behaviour that are damaging to themselves or others, but a recognition that all individuals with whom one works are human beings who are of supreme value in their own right, whatever they may have done, combined with a desire to assist them to be freed from whatever it is that imprisons or limits them, whether that be internal psychology or social context or both. With luck, such an attitude displayed by the psychotherapist provides sufficient safety for individuals to risk beginning to explore and acknowledge the whole of their personalities.

A God whose love is trusted to be inclusive of individuals' whole personalities, both good and evil, rather than selective and rejecting of their negative aspects, may enable believers to come to terms with the totality of their characters. As a consequence they will not need to resort to suppression or repression in order to be accepted, and thereby facilitate a positive transformation in their behaviour and attitudes. In contrast, *a God whose love is experienced as conditional can never bring about either psychological or spiritual healing. A God who loves conditionally, and who backs up his demands for conformity from believers with all manner of threatened punishments, can never bring about psychological integration in his followers.*

The Integration of the Shadow in Christian Spirituality

Fortunately, despite the negative effects of much orthodox doctrine and many traditional spiritual practices, much Christian spirituality demonstrates a concern to enable individuals to know themselves, and to come to terms with those aspects of their characters which they find difficult to recognise or value. In our attempts to integrate the Christian shadow, we need not rely exclusively on the psychotherapeutic tradition; we may also draw on these existing resources within the Christian spiritual tradition.

Confession is the practice that is most likely to stimulate a conscious recognition of the negative side of the personality. Even though there is a danger that, when wrongly used, it may encourage destructive forms of suppression or negative attitudes towards themselves amongst some penitents, for those believers who are beginning to have a *genuine* feeling of value and self-worth it can be very helpful, if conducted by a priest with psychological insight and sensitivity. For such people confession is a psychologically healthy and creative activity because they are encouraged to acknowledge those aspects of their characters which do not conform to the Christian ideal; in other words, to integrate them into their pictures of themselves, rather than either fighting or ignoring and forgetting them. As a result, the inner self is recognised as a mixture of positive and negative elements; in other words, a personal knowledge of good and evil develops. This enables believers to grow towards maturation, which involves the acceptance of ambiguity and a diminution in the use of repression as a defence. The result can be that, as well as gaining

self-acceptance, such penitents are much better able to recognise and tolerate the good and bad parts of other people and
to continue in positive relationships with them, even when
they behave in hurtful ways, although it must be conceded
that at times most of us do not have the strengh to continue in
relationship with people whose behaviour we find intolerable
and who will not change.

Another means by which traditional Christian spirituality
encourages the assimilation of the shadow is the practice of
meditation. One result of meditation is that those who meditate gradually learn to accept themselves and, thus, also other
people and God. As John Main explains:

> Meditation is the first step towards establishing the basic
> human relationship, the relationship with yourself.
> When you meditate, you do not try to please anyone.
> You do not try to respond to any role or any image of
> yourself. Perhaps we all do, to a certain extent, at the
> beginning. We see ourselves as some holy Buddha, about
> to levitate maybe. But you soon get over that once you
> start to meditate on a regular basis. The romantic under-
> standing of meditation soon gives way before the
> experience of the real thing. In fact, it is not only that you
> give up trying to respond to an image of yourself or
> someone else's image of yourself, but in meditating you
> let go of all images. You empty yourself of all images:
> that is what meditating is about. It is the process of
> emptying out of all the fantasy, all the images, all
> the unreality. So space is made for the real you, the real
> person you are. Here is a way of looking at meditation:
> it is a way of making space for yourself to be.
>
> In religious terms people often talk about loving God,
> loving your neighbour and loving yourself. But I think
> only a little experience with meditating will show you
> that the true order is the other way round. You must first
> learn to be yourself and to love yourself. And secondly
> you must allow your neighbour to be themselves and

learn to love them. And it is then, and only then, that it makes any sense to talk about God. And indeed, the less you talk and think about God in the initial stages, the better. (Main, 1989, pp. 57–8)

Authentic Christian spiritual practice enables those who pray and meditate to accept themselves and others as the people they happen to be. It enables the devout to grow in genuine love for self and others, and also to grow in an awareness of the love of God. Somehow mysteriously over time the practice of meditation and other forms of prayer results in a profound conviction that the one at the heart of the universe is good and beneficent, and this belief in itself makes it easier to relax and be honest with God and other people. Although Jung did not adequately acknowledge this, meditation encourages self-acceptance in a manner analogous to the integration of the shadow in Jungian psychotherapy. The conviction that this God is loving may enable people who meditate to risk becoming aware of the darkest facets of themselves. However, sometimes these can be so difficult to face that psychotherapeutic help may also be necessary.

A Spirituality of the Cross

In his book *The Crucified is no Stranger* (1977) Sebastian Moore, who is much influenced by Jung, presents an interpretation of the cross which is helpful in developing a spirituality which enables us to recognise both our desire for God and our resistance to his love without denying the reality of either. Moore explores the relationship between forgiveness and repentance and points out that:

Christianity is revolutionary. For it makes the death of Christ reconciliatory in the sense of making *God* convincing to *us*, of displacing for us the God of our fear. It makes it clear that it was *only* a question of opening *our minds and hearts* for God to appear. No question of placating *God*. It refers to the miraculous cessation of fear, and the consequent appearance of a totally new God, no longer the God we have seen filtered through the human nightmare. (Moore, 1977, p. 47, italics in original)

Moore proposes an interpretation of the crucifixion in which Christ is seen as the one who comes offering us total acceptance from God. However, we are so committed to being the centre of our own lives that we kill him.

He suggests a form of meditation on the crucifixion which will facilitate us in becoming conscious of our own evil, of which we are not normally aware:

> This consists in first becoming convinced of God's love as an all-penetrating force: then coming to experience evil in myself as a reality so pervasive and elusive as to its origin, that I cannot experience *it* as accepted by God in love without the presence of some other factor, in which God's love would *go to meet* my evil. This other factor is the crucifixion and death of Jesus, when this is regarded precisely as 'authorised' by God to declare his love for us. For in this conception, God obeys the deepest psychological law of acceptance: to be convinced of my acceptance, I must know that I am accepted at my worst. God shows me to myself as worse than I had ever conceived – a crucifier of the sinless one – in order to leave me in no possible room for doubt – that is to say no possible *further* experience of evil that might create doubt – that he loves and accepts me. (Moore, 1977, p. 4, italics in original)

In one and the same movement Christ discloses my evil at its worst (judgement) as being unable to destroy God's love for me (forgiveness) and this disclosure frees me to love in return (repentance), and the place where this revelation is made clear is the cross. However:

> *Liberation* from sin is rooted in the *forgiveness* of sin only when sin is understood as the tyranny of self-worship,

117

revealed in Christ as at root self-crucifixion, and resolved in the faithful vision of the crucified. In this ultimate form of forgiveness, in which *God* forgives, it is in the forgiven person, not in the pardoner, that 'relenting' happens. Thus the freedom which, in an interpersonal situation, is generally experienced more by the forgiver than the forgiven, in the divine forgiveness is wholly in the forgiven. We are let off from worshipping ourselves. God lets us off from worshipping ourselves, and so frees us for life. (Moore, 1977, p. 93, italics in original)

Moore's account is an extremely illuminating description of how the cross may be used positively in an individual's spiritual life as a means to facilitate both a belief in God's love and the integration of the shadow. He emphasises the paradox that we have crucified the one who represents the life that God gives us. In Christ we discover our potential wholeness, which is identical to our identity as a child and friend of God. However, we discover it not as a present possession, but as something that we have rejected and attempted to destroy. Even so, the discovery of what we have done opens up to us the possibility of ceasing to be a crucifier in so far as we accept the identity which Christ offers us. As we do so, we experience ourselves as crucified with Christ by the very actions through which we have been resisting God's love. We come to know ourselves as our own enemies as well as the enemies of God, but we also discover that God refuses to be our enemy.

If we adopt this perspective, we gradually come to recognise how much the approach of God towards us in love has been experienced through the filter of our own damaged psyches which may even have distorted it into a threat. We also become aware that *the appearance of Christ reveals how in many respects our religion is not a system of grace, but a structure of sin designed to defend ourselves against God, whilst at the same time giving us the delusion that we are in an intimate relationship with him when we are not*. In addition, we may begin to see how the wrathful and punitive depictions of God's behaviour in

118

the Bible and the Christian tradition incorporate projections of our own rage and aggression onto God, and that God is not like that. Because Sebastian Moore's spirituality of the cross provides us with a means of viewing the cross positively without attributing to God a rage which rejects us, it has the potential to encourage the development of a mature life of faith which is consistent with contemporary psychological insights into human development, and which assists in the integration of the shadow.

Refusing to Bow to the God of Group Belonging

The integration of the Christian shadow requires believers not only to acknowledge their own shadows and to abandon the attempt to boost themselves by regarding others as in some sense inferior or sinful, but also to give up the benefits of group conformity when this requires a sacrifice of the true self. These benefits are very great – group membership, acceptance, a sense of virtue or superiority, and so forth – but the price paid for these benefits may be even greater: the surrendering of important aspects of one's soul to the religious community, its ideology and the depiction of God which is believed to guarantee its values and virtue (the god of group belonging).

An essential stage in escaping from the god of group belonging is to recognise what it really means, and what it has cost you, to belong to the Church in this way. This process of discovery is very painful because it means re-evaluating your past behaviour and commitments and acknowledging that you were in many ways deceived by the ecclesiastical institution, by people within it whom you accepted as guides and, not least, by yourself and your unconscious motivations. It also means facing the emotional needs and immaturity that have led you to accept the compromises to your integrity entailed by membership of the Church and, in addition, risking rejection, because your greater self-awareness, changed beliefs and critique of the institution may well alienate those who are still committed to it.

One of the implications of Jesus' encounters with the sinful, the poor and the outcast is that those who are outside the official structures of religion and 'the community of the elect' may be better able to hear the gospel than those who fulfil the requirements of authorised religion. This is a paradox which crops up frequently in the Gospels: *the religious outsiders, regarded as sinners by the insiders, are much better able to hear the message of Jesus than those with impeccable religious credentials.* Indeed, it is precisely their devotion to the divine Law that prevents the Pharisees and others from responding. The outsiders have nothing to rely on except the unexpected grace of God and are, therefore, able to respond to it – as the 'sinners' in the Gospels demonstrate. In contrast, those who are 'on the inside' are very likely to have bought into the conditions that organised religion lays down for acceptance by God and, therefore, to be deaf to the words that Christ speaks to them.

One way in which the process of resistance to the god of group belonging may be facilitated is by taking seriously the possibility that God may be found amongst the excluded, and by listening to those who are outside the 'righteous' group. Paul Minear's commentary on the Parable of the Sheep and the Goats (Matthew 25:31–46) gives guidance about how we may recognise the presence of God in places where conventional religion is unable to acknowledge it. According to Minear, the parable is answering a question about how the Lord may be known now that he is no longer present in the body:

> He visits us as 'one of the least of these' ... Jesus' parable does not measure leastness in terms of economic destitution alone, but includes social ostracism as well. There are sick people; in the Bible sickness connotes sin and contagion. There are naked people; in the Bible nakedness connotes guilt and disgrace. More important still, the parable mentions aliens and convicts. The *least*

are folk who are ostracised, who possess no significance, prestige or power. Matthew and his first readers would have included wandering Christian prophets, imprisoned by their enemies (10:16–23; 24:9–14). To visit *them* in prison makes one a social deviate, an offence to respectable folk. To identify oneself with them is to share all the hostility and danger in which they stood. (Minear, 1984, p. 181, italics in original)

Christ is found in 'the least of these', and if we separate ourselves by making moral distinctions between them and us, we separate ourselves from him. (The same is true if we act out of a self-conscious conviction that we are caring for Christ by caring for them. That is just another way of boosting our sense of moral worth.) If Christians can come to terms with this truth, it may be possible for them to learn from those whom they have previously rejected.

The invitation which outcasts extend to conventional Christians is to recognise that the comfort provided by a sense of belonging is a delusion, that they too are in exile. As John Fortunato says:

We are *all* in one way or another, in exile. We are all 'not home'. That is the plight of us creatures in this post-Resurrection, pre-Parousia situation. Whether one is black or a woman, divorced, handicapped, damaged from childhood abuse, a teenager, or a person with AIDS (no matter how one contracted it), we have all tasted the abyss. (Fortunato, 1987, p. 33)

The reason why this is not obvious to all Christians is that the gospel has often been perverted into a support for the *status quo* and the fearful ego, rather than being a source of hope for the exile. Paradoxically, it is the exile who discovers in the experience of rejection by other people that God accepts him or her as he or she is. Because the Church usually prefers security to exile, and a good name to identification with the outcast, it has failed to enter into this experience. When the

Church has identified itself with the authority of Jesus, rather than accepting that it belongs to this fallen world, in whose limitations and sin it shares, it has tempered its response to the outcast with a moralism which is contrary to the gospel, but which has nevertheless been advanced in the name of the gospel. Only if all of us in the Church, as well as the ecclesiastical institutions to which we belong, abandon our moral superiority and recognise that we too are in exile, will we be able truly to witness to the God who accepts 'the least of these'. *Ultimately, all that we in the Church are is a collection of exiles who are loved by God in our sinful and vulnerable humanity and who seek to respond, however inadequately, to his love.*

CHAPTER FIVE

Theological Uncertainty and the Reform of the Church

The Shadow of the Church

In addition to the integration of the shadows of individual Christians, the Church as a collective body needs to recognise and assimilate its own shadow. According to the Gospels, the chief opponents of Jesus were the religious leaders of the Jews. This is no coincidence because, as I have argued, they were defending a conception of religious truth, the Law, which was necessarily opposed to the unconditional love of God which Jesus communicated. The hierarchies of contemporary churches very often promote forms of Christian spirituality and belief that substitute a new kind of Law for the transformation which is promised by the gospel. They act as the guardians of the gods of group belonging of the ideological communities to which their denominations are assimilated, and seek to enforce conformity to the diktats of those gods upon their members. Only if the churches cease both to identify the God of Jesus Christ with the god of group belonging, and themselves as institutions in one way or another with the truth and authority of God, will the integration of their shadows become possible.

There is an ambiguity about the Church's ability to bring people into relationship with God which has not been sufficiently acknowledged by the institutional churches and mainstream Christian teaching: although it claims to be the Body of Christ and the People of God and to possess the revealed truth about God, the Church (by which I mean the sum of all ecclesiastical bodies claiming belief in Christ) is made up of human institutions functioning in very human ways, and subject to the ordinary cultural influences that shape all human societies. Many of the troubles of church bodies arise from their failure adequately to recognise that they cannot escape from these conditioning factors and, consequently, that the religious affirmations which they make about themselves and their teachings are often severely compromised.

Instead of admitting the provisional and culturally conditioned nature of their knowledge of God, and despite formulaic liturgical attestations of individual sinfulness, the churches generally act as if they were in some way insulated by the Holy Spirit from the sins, errors and contingency that are the ordinary lot of humankind. Consequently, they often make arrogant and false claims that prevent both themselves as organisations and many of their members from engaging on the journey of genuine spiritual transformation. Very often churchgoers identify their form of Christian belief or the ecclesiastical institution to which they belong with the authority and truth of God. This enables them, on the one hand, with apparent humility to assert that they are sinners and fallible whilst, on the other hand, gaining a sense of certainty and spiritual superiority because they belong to a religious community which, they genuinely believe, possesses the truth about God. This is a form of the spirituality of identification, which I have already described. As in the case of ideological closure, it is a shortcut enabling individual Christians or communities to claim God's favour for themselves and to justify their lifestyles and values with the authority of Christ. However, this identification is false. The problem is that no Christians are, nor ever can be, truly or completely good and none have unambiguous knowledge of the truth and, in addition, ecclesiastical institutions, as recent scandals demonstrate, are every bit as open to error and sin as individual believers. Consequently, those who adopt a spirituality of identification can only maintain it by repressing or denying unacceptable aspects of their institutions or of their own characters or behaviour, along with their questions and doubts, or by scapegoating others for their own failings. As a result vast amounts of emotional energy are used by church leaders and members to maintain a false appearance of virtue and knowledge, with dire consequences for both their spiritual and psychological growth.

Sexual Abuse in the Roman Catholic Church

The present scandals which are afflicting a number of the churches show how serious the results of this strategy can be, especially that afflicting the Roman Catholic Church concerning child sexual abuse by a number of its clergy. I am writing this section as the Roman Catholic hierarchy in Ireland and, in particular, its leader, Cardinal Desmond Connell, Archbishop of Dublin, are in the midst of a scandal concerning the sexual abuse of children by clergy. A programme, called *Cardinal Secrets*, produced by RTE, the state-owned television company, revealed several cases in which priests, whom the hierarchy of the Dublin archdiocese knew to have abused children, were reassigned to parishes or institutions where they had further access to children. In addition, the receiving local authorities with responsibility for these priests were not informed of their past offences. Instead of involving the police, the Church used its own internal procedures and its code of Canon Law to deal with these allegations, setting itself apart from normal professional good practice and the legal requirement to report current sexual abuse that applies in secular society; and these clergy subsequently continued to molest children. Whereas Cardinal Connell has apologised for his failings in handling these matters, the outrage in Ireland at his alleged covering up of the abuse is very great and there are calls for his resignation or prosecution. The Church appears to have put its own interests as an institution before those of the actual and potential child victims of its priests.

Of course, Ireland is not alone in the Roman Catholic Church in recent years in witnessing the emergence of numerous allegations of sexual abuse by clergy, and a failure by the church authorities to act to protect victims. Frequently, offenders have been sent to other pastoral positions with access to children and the secular authorities have not been told about the criminal actions of these priests. A good example is the Archdiocese of Boston in the United States where Cardinal Bernard Law has been forced to resign because of his reassignment of sexually abusive priests to pastoral positions. There appears to be an institutional malaise afflicting the Roman Catholic Church worldwide that has made it possible for these serious errors of judgement to occur.

One reason why such misjudgements have proliferated is the priority that has been given by the Catholic bishops to Canon Law, the Church's own legal code, over that of the laws of the countries in which it is located. I heard one priest interviewed on the radio asserting that Canon Law was the law of God and that it took priority over state laws. This view is very ancient and was a source of dispute between secular rulers and the Church as far back as the Middle Ages. For example, in England at the time of Henry II the clergy came under the jurisdiction of special church courts and were only handed over to the secular courts for trial in the case of high treason. This was one of the major causes of Henry's dispute with his Archbishop of Canterbury, Thomas à Becket, who opposed the king's intention to bring 'criminous clerks' under secular jurisdiction. This special treatment was also a source of resentment against the clergy in the general population, especially since the church courts tended to give much milder punishments than the secular ones (Moorman, 1963, pp. 76–81). It seems that the issue which led to Becket's death eight hundred years ago has still not been resolved: the Catholic Church still believes that it should not be answerable to the secular law.

The ecclesiastical identification of the Church with the knowledge and authority of God lies behind the existence of these two parallel systems of law. This identification reminds me of the ancient Christian heresy called Docetism, which stated that Jesus was fully divine but only appeared to be human. Much of the theology of the Church contains Docetic assumptions which implicitly suggest that it is not really human and not subject to the same constraints as the rest of the human race. This theology also gives expression to the fundamental dualism at the heart of orthodox Christianity. As we have seen, polarised or dualistic thinking is built into the foundations of the normative teaching of the Christian religion as the eternal division between the elect and the reprobate, but it occurs in numerous other forms. These have in common the characteristic that the Church as an institution, or those holding leadership within it, or individual Christians, are identified in some way with the holy, the true or the superior, whereas someone else is identified with evil, error or inferiority. Those who are holy attract God's favour and those who are not, his rejection or punishment.

When, as a result of this dualistic thinking, the Church as an institution is identified with the authority of God, the conditions are created in which, ultimately, it becomes possible for members of the hierarchy to think it proper and appropriate for them not to inform the secular police about child sexual abuse by serving priests, because they are following the procedures of their own code of Canon Law, which protects the confidentiality of their diocesan files. In my view, the alleged behaviour of Cardinal Connell, Cardinal Law and other members of the Catholic hierarchy only becomes explicable when one recognises that they were acting out of a belief that the rules that apply to other mortals in our society do not apply to them. It is clearly the underlying assumption that makes sense of their misjudgements. And this belief arises from the identification in Catholic doctrine of the Catholic Church with the authority of Christ.

The Roman Catholic Church claims privileged access to the

truth about God. It asserts that it possesses the Magisterium, the right to define the nature of Christian doctrine given to the papacy by God and, in particular circumstances, it attributes infallibility to the declarations of the Pope. It also claims that its sacraments guarantee the presence of God in a special way and that it has the right to give or withhold absolution for sins. In the past, it also asserted that there was 'no salvation outside the Church' and, hence, that all those who died out of communion with the Catholic Church were damned. The Second Vatican Council modified these claims somewhat, but still placed the pope at the centre of the relationship between the Church and God and only admitted other Christian denominations, let alone other religions, to a secondary and inferior relationship to the truth about God (Abbott, 1966, pp. 14–101).

These doctrinal positions clearly demonstrate an identification of the Roman Catholic Church with the authority of God. The very title of the pope, the Vicar of Christ, indicates this. He stands in the place of Christ in this world and exercises the functions of teaching and leadership within the Christian community, 'the Body of Christ' and 'the People of God', in other words, the new Chosen People, on his behalf. This attitude leads the Church to become puffed up with its own importance and makes it unable to give due weight to the opinions of those who disagree with it, whether inside or outside its boundaries, or to recognise its own failings. It also produces a power drive. After all, if the Church has a unique relationship with God and its leader represents Christ, it is the only source of genuine knowledge about ultimate reality in this world. It follows that there is no other perspective that can have equal validity with its own. Thus, the Catholic Church does not need to listen to others; they must listen to it! Because of this conviction, over the centuries the Roman Catholic Church has frequently functioned as an ideologically closed institution, a tendency that is today encouraged by the conservative and centralising policies of the present pope, John Paul II. Historically, the Roman Catholic Church has often been guilty of power-driven and abusive behaviour, such as the torture and execution of heretics. It should come as no surprise that an institution which has been capable of so many past offences against humanity should still be subject to modes of thinking and behaviour that are intrinsically abusive.

Despite decades of ecumenical discussions, these exclusive attitudes do not appear to be weakening. If anything, they are hardening. In 1998 the Catholic bishops in the British Isles issued a document, *One Bread One Body*, which restated the traditional ban on Catholics from receiving communion in Protestant churches and on Protestants from receiving communion in Catholic churches, except in very limited circumstances and *in extremis*. It also affirmed the teaching of the papal bull, *Apostolicae Curae*, of 1896 which declared Anglican orders invalid (McGarry, 2001). Furthermore, in September 2000:

> The Vatican published the document *Dominus Iesus* which dismissed all Protestant denominations as 'not Churches in the proper sense' and all other religions as being 'in a gravely deficient situation'. A letter sent by Rome to Catholic bishops worldwide around the same time instructed them not to refer to Protestant Churches as 'sister Churches'. (McGarry, 2001)

At the popular level, this exclusive and exalted teaching about the Catholic Church may give rise to a totally uncritical attitude towards the Church which goes well beyond even its own doctrines about itself, and displays the Docetic tendency very clearly. For example, one correspondent to the editor of the Irish newspaper the *Sunday Independent* wrote the following in reaction to the criticism of Cardinal Connell by one of its journalists, Emer O'Kelly:

> This institution (the Catholic Church), like its founder, is divine. It is impeccable, cannot err and is going to be around until the end of time. Miss O'Kelly will have to

live with that. She must realise that many of those who are members of the institution are corrupt – not the institution itself. Right through her article she puts the prefix 'Roman' before Catholic when referring to the Catholic Church, its religion and members. This is incorrect. It is also grammatically wrong. Catholic means 'universal'. One cannot limit the unlimited or localise the universal. (Dowling, 2002)

A religious system that produces views about itself such as those quoted provides the perfect conditions in which the spiritual abuse of its members can occur. The seduction or rape of children represents the extreme case of spiritual abuse, but it could not have taken place in the way in which it did if the Catholic priesthood had not been held in such high esteem, even idealised, by the population, in general, and by the teaching of the Church, in particular. The trust of parents and children in their priests, who were regarded as different from other men, was taken advantage of by that minority who wished to prey upon young people. In the vast majority of cases the children who were their victims said nothing about it until they were adults and, even in the cases in which they did, their parents either could not or would not believe them or, if they did, found it very difficult to get an adequate response from the church authorities to their allegations.

In fairness, it should be noted that in Ireland covering up the sexual abuse of children has not only been practised by the Catholic hierarchy. Sexual abuse has been extremely common in Irish society in general, and it is mentioned frequently in the consulting-room. Furthermore, sexual abuse, let alone other prohibited sexual behaviour, such as promiscuity, homosexuality and adultery, has not been limited solely to the clergy of the Catholic Church either in Ireland or elsewhere. Nevertheless, the inculcation of an uncritical conformity and acceptance of church teaching in Catholics, combined with the extraordinary dominance of the Roman Catholic Church over Irish society from the time of independence until a few years ago, made it very difficult for Irish Catholics to ask questions about, let alone challenge, the actions of the Church or its priests.

The combination of institutional power with such deference has made it difficult for the Catholic hierarchy to scrutinise itself or to see the situation from the perspective of those outside the clerical caste. It is very easy for the clergy to identify themselves with their religious role and thereby to lose their sense of who they really are as individual sinful people, especially if they have been in training since their teenage years. It is also easy for the Church as an institution to identify with its own teaching about itself. Whenever such identification occurs, the priests or ecclesiastical institutions concerned lose something of their humanity and may, at least unconsciously, regard themselves as different in significant ways from the rest of the human race.

They may also, as the Jungian analyst Adolph Guggenbühl-Craig (1971) suggests, become more concerned with power than with truth. Of course, this development is often a feature of organisations, but the natural tendency of the Catholic hierarchy to defend the Church against potential scandal and criticism is strongly reinforced by the identification of the Catholic Church with the authority of Christ. This identification appears to lie behind the failure of so many Roman Catholic bishops to hand over abusive clergy to the secular police and courts. It led them to give more importance to the Church's own internal laws, and to the preservation of its reputation and privileged place in Irish and American society, than to the protection of children. One can only conclude that, *far from being the result of the sinfulness or misjudgement of individuals, the failure of the Catholic Church in Ireland and elsewhere to deal adequately with its sexually abusive priests is a natural, possibly inevitable, consequence of the deep assumptions that provide the foundations for its existence as a religious system.*

Sexual Abuse and Hypocrisy in Other Churches

The Roman Catholic Church's assumptions about itself as an

131

institution are more extreme than those of most other churches. However, there are no grounds for other churches to be complacent. The danger is that non-Catholics may scapegoat the Roman Catholic Church for tendencies and errors of which we are all guilty, even if in less obvious ways. It is normal for ecclesiastical bodies to fear scandal, and to be intent upon appearing better in public than they are in private. In general, the churches choose to hide their faults when they can. Fewer accusations of the sexual abuse of children may have been made in non-Catholic churches than in the Catholic Church, but there is considerable evidence of sexual abuse within pastoral relationships with adults. Recently, a report was produced in Britain on the behaviour of clergy in the mainstream denominations towards women members of their congregations, which alleged that there was a widespread cover-up of this problem in the Anglican as well as some other churches (reported in the *Guardian*, 26 July 2003).

It is clear that churches other than the Roman Catholic have been guilty of moving ministers who are incompetent, mentally unbalanced or guilty of abusive or potentially or actually scandalous behaviour to other congregations, often without informing their new colleagues or parishioners of their past actions or present failings. They have also adopted the belief that it is better for them to appear to be good than for their sinfulness or human inadequacy to be publicly known or acknowledged. Except in a liturgical context, and without mentioning any specific sinful deeds, it is rare for the churches as institutions to follow the example in the Paraable of the Tax Collector and confess that they are sinful and in need of the mercy of God. Even when they do, it is likely to be late in the day; for example, it took the Church of Ireland 150 years to apologise for abuses which took place during the Irish potato famine in the 1840s.

Very often church institutions have identified themselves with the message which they preach rather than recognising that the gospel is not something which they possess, but something to which they witness, attempting to communicate its real but elusive existence to the world. The truth is that the gospel comes first as judgement upon the Church, and only when the Church receives the judgement and acknowledges the need to change does it actually begin to display to the world something of the transformed life promised by Jesus. Whilst it refuses the judgement and claims a false identification between itself and the things of God, the Church is condemned to a future in which it repetitiously substitutes pretence for reality and lies for truth. Only if the ecclesiastical establishment faces its own shadow and consistently teaches its members that the Church is always and inevitably a gathering of sinners, not of the virtuous, will a genuine reform of the Church become possible.

Identification and the Defence of Literalism

The integration of the shadow of the Church will be much assisted by a recognition that no Christian group possesses the exclusive or definitive truth about Christ. Identifications of the teachings of particular Christian bodies with the revealed truth about God provide spurious and extremely dangerous support and justification for the power drives of the communities who claim them. In order to see why these identifications are unjustifiable we will consider mainstream Christian beliefs about the Bible and revelation. Traditional Christianity, although it acknowledges the truth that from an ordinary human point of view we do not know God as he is in himself, seeks to get around this difficulty by using the idea of revelation: God makes himself known in specific actions and in the words of the Bible, and he inspires the teachings of the Church. Roman Catholics are not alone amongst Christians in identifying their beliefs with the divinely guaranteed truth; most, if not all, Christian denominations claim a special authority for their doctrinal positions on the basis that God has revealed himself through Jesus Christ, and that that revelation is in some manner contained in the Bible. In their different ways they use a belief in revelation to isolate a

133

particular source of religious knowledge from the finite and conditioned world of ordinary human experience and, thus, attempt to guarantee the truths it asserts against the limitations and relativity of all merely human perception and thought.

This manoeuvre sets up a division between two different sources of knowledge – revelation, on the one hand, and human experience and reflection, on the other – which is the origin of the conflict between the Christian religion and science. The *genuine* distinction between the visible tangible created realm and the hidden intangible realm of the divine mystery is brought down to earth and made the grounds of a *false* distinction between different aspects of human experience, including a separation between the 'sacred' realm of the Church and the 'secular' realm of 'the world'. This dualism is replicated in an extensive series of oppositions in Christian thinking between the things of God and those that are merely human, including that between 'the saved' and 'the damned' which is so important in sustaining the Christian complex. In various ways the churches have identified themselves and their teachings with the authority and truth of God and, over the centuries, they have protected those identifications by the denial of alternative perspectives, the repression of doubt, ideological closure, the silencing of dissent, and persecution: practices which have encouraged the anxiety that drives the complex. If the churches are to be rid of abusive and authoritarian structures, it will be necessary to reconfigure Christian doctrine so that the identifications of themselves or the Bible with divine authority and truth are dissolved.

Amongst Protestants, the belief of many conservative Evangelicals in the inerrancy of the Bible is an example of such an identification. This belief is structurally analogous to that of Roman Catholics in the papacy, though the content is different. In this case, the conduit of absolute truth is located in the text of the Bible itself, which is claimed to be both inspired by God and guaranteed by him to be free from error. It is identified with, and referred to as, 'the Word of God'. The claim to inerrancy puts the Bible outside the contingent realm. However, such a view of the Bible has become unsustainable in the light of contemporary biblical scholarship, which has demonstrated that in many respects the Bible is neither literally true nor historically accurate, and that both its creation and its historical interpretation have been very much subject to cultural conditioning, ideological influences and even deliberate distortion.

If Christian belief is to be maintained there has to be a way of talking credibly about the inspiration of the Bible in the light of the results of such biblical research. In other words, we need to be able to show how God speaks to us through the Bible without resorting to identification or ideological closure in order to do so. The problem is that there is no universally accepted or definitive method of doing this, although different people resolve this difficulty in different ways to their own satisfaction. Often students of the Bible have become disillusioned with critical scholarship because it appears to have destroyed the possibility of accepting the divine inspiration of the Scriptures and, hence, also of the teachings of the Church that are based upon the Scriptures. This problem arises because there is an apparent incompatibility between a view of the Bible as the revealed and inspired Word of God and the discovery of many inconsistencies and historical inaccuracies within it. And it is compounded by the realisation that the Bible was not produced solely by the Holy Spirit's direct inspiration of its original authors, but by processes of oral and written transmission and by the editing of texts over several generations. Of course, these may also have been inspired, but many Christians find it difficult to change their model of the inspiration of the Bible from one of direct verbal inspiration, i.e. dictation, by the Holy Spirit to one in which God works over decades or centuries through these much more diffuse and drawn-out processes.

Since the historical truth of the Bible can no longer be taken for granted, but has to be established by historical analysis, the religious authority of the Bible is also put into question. *If it cannot be trusted to be historically accurate, how can it be trusted to give accurate guidance to the mysteries of faith or be accepted as a genuine revelation from God?* This poses a particular problem since Christianity is an historical religion and bases its claim to be able to communicate the truth about God on the belief that God has revealed himself in particular historical events, especially the history of the Jews and the life, death and resurrection of Jesus of Nazareth. If the historicity of these events is put in doubt, their religious significance is also open to question. Thus, if the historicity of the resurrection is questioned, leaving open the possibility that Jesus is still lying in a tomb somewhere in Israel, the religious claim that he has risen from the dead and made it possible for those who believe in him to have eternal life also becomes questionable and, for many people, preposterous. Likewise, if scholars argue that the Evangelists edited their accounts of Jesus to meet the needs of particular communities and that they embellished various stories to make a particular point, the idea that they were inspired whilst writing the Gospels becomes dubious. Even their veracity as historical witnesses becomes open to question.

Even for someone who does not believe that the Bible is without error, but is convinced that it is inspired by the Spirit of God, there is a problem in reconciling these academic conclusions with the belief that what the Bible says about God is true. Like peeling the proverbial onion, scholarship has stripped away the layers of historical and cultural conditioning until there seems to be nothing left in the Bible that can be attributed unequivocally to the activity of God, no assured authority and no certain content of belief. The critical approach fails to provide an adequate support for a Christian account of life because it is often reductive, and the historical record by itself does not provide religious significance. *It is the interpretation of history from the perspective of faith that is religiously significant, and historical criticism appears to put this in doubt.*

Since Christians experience their faith as putting them in

relationship to God and fulfilling many of their most fundamental spiritual, emotional and social needs, they have a very
strong motivation to defend it against those who appear to be
suggesting that it is in error. Unfortunately, they may do so by
getting so defensive that they close themselves off from a genuine encounter and exchange with the questions raised by
those with an opposing point of view; in other words, by
resorting to ideological closure. They may reassert the truth of
the biblical revelation and denigrate the critical scholarship
that has put its authority in question. Like White settlers
attacked by Red Indians in a Western film, such Christians
draw their wagons into a circle and defend themselves from
the possibility of a creative engagement not only with biblical
scholarship, but also with contemporary culture in general.
The more threatened they are, the more tightly do they close
ranks and refuse to listen to the voices of academic critics or
the questions of ordinary people. They perceive these as the
siren songs of those who have sold out to secular perspectives
calling them onto the rocks of relativism and disbelief. Hence,
they cut themselves off from any constructive or fertile
engagement with modern thought. In this way, many devout
Christians adopt forms of Christian belief that are anti-
intellectual and are only sustained through the exclusion
of concepts and persons who do not conform to what they
proclaim. The resulting type of religious belief is a form
of fanaticism. As Jung says:

> Fanaticism is always a sign of repressed doubt. You can
> study that in the history of the Church. Always in those
> times when the Church begins to waver the style
> becomes fanatical, or fanatical sects spring up, because
> the secret doubt has to be quenched. When one is really
> convinced, one is perfectly calm and can discuss one's
> belief as a personal point of view without any particular
> resentment. (Jung, 1935/1977, p. 154, para. 355)

At the extreme, this mode of defence gives birth to *funda-
mentalism*, the belief in the absolute literal truth of every word

of the Bible, its inerrancy. In essence, *the belief in biblical inerrancy isolates the Bible from the conditioning and corrupting influences of a fallen world: its truth is guaranteed by God.* This belief is another example of the Docetic tendency. The Bible is regarded not as a product of normal human creative processes, but as a special creation of God. The human element seems to have been completely overridden by divine intervention. This is why those who assert inerrancy reject the historical and critical method of studying the Bible which is used in most university faculties of theology. Indeed, their general strategy is to make the Bible the first authority in all matters.

This results in a curious methodology: only those matters on which the Bible does not comment are permitted to be viewed through an empirical lens, and where there is a conflict between the Bible and empirical studies, the teachings of the Bible must take precedence. The Bible is to be trusted above the evidence of the senses or the explorations of scholars or scientists. This leads to some absurd inconsistencies. For example, a Creationist, one who rejects the theory of evolution and believes that Adam and Eve were the first human beings, may accept the theory of relativity, even though the empirical method which lies behind the two theories is in principal the same. Strangely, however, Creationists usually do not also maintain that the Earth is the static centre of the universe and that the Sun circles it, although that is what the Bible says. Indeed, it was the denial of this belief that led Galileo to be condemned by the Inquisition, precisely because he thereby contradicted the clear teaching of the Bible (Sobel, 1999, pp. 76–8).

An identification of the Bible with the authority and truth of God lies behind the beliefs of Creationists. Conservative Christians usually also make this identification, at least to a significant degree, even when they do not regard the Bible as actually inerrant. A similar identification, but in this case of the teaching of the Church with the authority and truth of God, is found amongst Roman Catholics who regard the declarations of the pope when speaking *ex cathedra* as infallible and, more generally, Christians who believe that the Church's teaching, especially that contained in the Ecumenical Creeds, gives inspired and assured knowledge of the truth about God. The belief that God speaks to us through the Bible is foundational of all but the most radical forms of Christian conviction, but when this belief results in such identifications, it provides essential support to the dualism of the Christian religion. These identifications divide the world of experience into natural and divine realms and are part of the split between the secular and the sacred which underlies power-driven, controlling and abusive behaviour within the institutional churches. Only when these are dissolved will the churches be able to look honestly at themselves and the world, and be able to acknowledge the unavoidable human limitations upon their knowledge and authority. Until this happens, they are condemned to live in the defensive corrals of ideological closure, hypocrisy and clerical control.

Sin and the Knowledge of God

Paradoxically, whilst claiming to possess a revelation from God, from very early in the history of the Church, theology has recognised that human beings can never achieve conceptual knowledge of God. This is because in essence *true knowledge of God is experiential knowledge: it is not attained by intellectual reflection, but only through the union of the soul with God through faith, hope and love.* In the early Church, holiness was regarded as an essential attribute of the theologian because sin distorts the vision of God. It is only the person who is truly guided by the Holy Spirit who can understand what God seeks to communicate of himself through the Bible. Theology grows out of a continuing relationship with God, and thus, if there is none, a person cannot be a theologian. For this reason the theologian has to be a person of prayer. A secular theologian is a contradiction in terms.

The Bible can only be correctly understood by one who is

illuminated by the Holy Spirit. The consequence of this position is that unless we are sure that we are inspired by the Holy Spirit, we can have no certainty that our understanding of the Bible is a true interpretation of what God intended to reveal about himself through its pages. However, the only evidence we have that any person is inspired by the Holy Spirit is his or her pattern of living. We must assume that those who continue to live lives that fall short of the Christian ideal, which of course includes ourselves, are in some way not in touch with, or failing to co-operate with, or actually resisting the purifying activity of the Spirit. At any rate, they are not yet fully in tune with the Spirit's intentions for them. It is reasonable, therefore, to say that only those who show evidence of true conversion of life can be presumed to be inspired by the Holy Spirit and, hence, that only those who are genuinely transformed have grounds for claiming to 'know' the meaning of what God has revealed of himself. It follows from this that *a claim to know the meaning of the Bible is also implicitly a claim to sanctity.* Any Christians who acknowledge themselves to be sinners must also acknowledge that they do not have access to the definitive meaning of the Bible. Since all Christians repeatedly confess that they are sinners, both in liturgical worship and private prayer, it follows that *no Christians can claim with integrity to be able to interpret the Bible truly and definitively.* To do so would amount to saying that they are in perfect accord with the Holy Spirit and no longer sin. We are all sinners. How then is it possible for any Christians to assert that their interpretation of the Bible is the assured truth about God? *Even if the Bible is objectively the revealed Word of God, none of us can be certain that we know what the definitive meaning of that revelation is!* To read the Bible with this awareness may enable the churches and individual Christians to behave with greater humility, and to avoid the false identification of their teachings with the guaranteed truth about God.

This conclusion, I believe, applies to office holders in the Church as much as to everyone else. The Catholic tradition of theology has recognised the individual fallibility of believers when they seek to understand the Bible, but it has sought to overcome this difficulty by asserting that the Church as a whole possesses the ability to arrive at authoritative interpretations, either through a general council of bishops or, in the Roman Catholic Church, the *ex cathedra* declarations of the pope. Indeed, the tendency of individuals to arrive at 'erroneous' or 'heterodox' conclusions is a major reason why Catholic theology promotes the Church's 'universal' teaching as a protection against the devout going astray. However, this procedure fails to take adequate account of the sinfulness of either office holders or the churches as institutions. In my view, it does not make any sense to recognise that every person in the Church, whether high or low in the hierarchy, whether lay or ordained, is a sinner and yet to claim that somehow the Holy Spirit is able to work perfectly through particular individuals, at particular times, merely because they happen to have been consecrated as bishops or elected as pope, especially in the light of the strong influence of both ideology and political leaders upon the Church and its hierarchy over the centuries. The more I have had to do with ecclesiastical officials and church committees, of whatever denomination, the more absurd this claim has come to appear to me. Being the Pope, the Archbishop of Canterbury, a council of bishops, a synod or a presbytery is no guarantee of being genuinely guided by the Spirit of God, a conclusion which is supported by the frequent and manifold disagreements between such bodies throughout Christian history. Even so, because they express the common mind of significant parts of the Church, their conclusions should be given serious consideration and not simply dismissed by those who disagree with them.

The Theology of Unknowing

Ironically, our inability to know the assured truth about God is recognised by some of the most conservative traditions of Christian theology, but the implications of this recognition for

141

the Christian religion as a whole have not been consistently followed through. There is an ancient distinction between two forms of theology: cataphatic and apophatic. The *cataphatic* or positive way proceeds by making affirmations about God. The *apophatic* or negative way proceeds by saying what God is not, or by speaking paradoxically. For most people and church communities most of the time, cataphatic theology is the normal way of reflecting on the Christian religion.

To say that God is good or loving or that Jesus is the Son of God, and that he died and rose again, are all affirmative statements. Most religious teaching takes this form in the Christian Church, and it is necessary that it does so in order to meet the psychological and educational needs of believers. Since we are finite contingent creatures who live in a world of physical sensations and perceptions, we need to have our ideas about God expressed in terms which we can relate to our sensations and perceptions. These are frequently rather concrete in nature. Most people find abstract thinking difficult and uninteresting. It does not move them. Far more effective in arousing spiritual devotion and involvement are images of God drawn from everyday experience. To refer to God as 'the unmoved prime mover' does little to excite most people, whereas to call him 'father', 'mother', 'lover', 'friend' or, even, 'judge' may touch their hearts. It means something to which they can relate.

In general, spiritual life begins with the communication of such accessible images of God and is nourished by reflection upon them. However, there is a danger in using such images of God. Since the divinity cannot be adequately represented by any of them, they are only limited and partial expressions of the mystery which we call God. The danger is that believers may come to treat these images as if they were true and final representations of the nature of the divinity, and refuse to consider any alternative depictions. This is what appears to have happened to those Christians who engage in a quest for certainty, or who treat the Bible as a literal and inerrant account of God's revelation in Christ.

Apophatic theology is the intellectual foundation of the

Christian tradition of contemplative or mystical spirituality, some of the best-known exponents of which include: St Gregory of Nyssa; Pseudo-Dionysius the Areopagite; the author of *The Cloud of Unknowing*; Meister Eckhart; St John of the Cross; and Thomas Merton. This theological tradition uses negative or paradoxical language to refer to God. For example, God may be described, negatively, as unlimited, unknowable or uncreated or, paradoxically, as three and one or as first and last. Such negative or paradoxical descriptions of God puzzle the human intellect, and should ensure that it does not fall into the delusion that it has understood, or can ever understand, the mystery of God. To describe God as unlimited, unknowable or uncreated does not tell us anything about the nature of God as such. Instead, it defines God as outside the realm of direct human experience and comprehension. To say that God is three and one or first and last is to contradict the normal categories of human thought and to invite Christians to stretch their ordinary ways of thinking to their extremes, and then a bit further, until they break down in the recognition that it is impossible to make rational sense of the mystery of God.

The great Orthodox theologian Vladimir Lossky describes Pseudo-Dionysius' theology thus:

> Dionysius distinguishes two possible theological ways. One – that of cataphatic or positive theology – proceeds by affirmations; the other – apophatic or negative theology – by negations. The first leads to some knowledge of God, but is an imperfect way. The perfect way, the only way which is fitting in regard to God, who is of His very nature unknowable, is the second – which leads us finally to total ignorance. All knowledge has as its object that which is. Now God is beyond all that exists. In order to approach Him it is necessary to deny all that is inferior to Him, that is to say, all that which is. If in seeing God one can know what one sees, then one has not seen God in Himself but something intelligible, something which

is inferior to Him. It is by *unknowing* ... that one may know Him who is above every possible object of knowledge. (Lossky, 1957, p. 25, italics in original)

This way of talking about God is by no means intended to suggest that God does not exist, but to emphasise that the mode of his existence is of a completely different order from that of the creation. God is not like the created order and cannot be known in the same way that we know the created order. Because this is the case, anything that we think we know in the normal culturally and psychologically conditioned manner of perceiving, whether sensory or imaginative, is not God, and any assertions that we make about God can never be true descriptions of what he is like. Put simply, the apophatic approach recognises that, because of the inability of human language to depict the eternal and uncreated, *all our statements about God are limited human constructions that can never truly describe God.*

The Metaphorical Nature of Religious Language

This conclusion helps us to recover an awareness of the true nature of theology which has been obscured by those Christians who have sought an illegitimate certainty for their religious convictions. Far from providing certainty, for centuries orthodox Christian teaching has acknowledged the limitations of the language we use to describe God. Religious language is essentially and irreducibly metaphorical. This has been recognised since at least the thirteenth century when St Thomas Aquinas, the greatest of Catholic theologians, argued that 'words are used of God metaphorically' (Aquinas, 1964, 1a; 13, 3). In religious language the unknown God is described in terms derived from human experience and can be described in *no other way*. Since we have to speak in terms derived from the everyday observable world in order to say anything at all about the invisible unconditioned nature of God, there is no direct or literal speech about God; all speech about God is essentially and irreducibly metaphorical.

Metaphors speak of one thing in terms of another; in other words, *as if* they were the same thing. For example, the Christian tradition speaks of God using the metaphor of 'father', depicting God as if he were a human father, even though he is not one. The characteristics associated with a human father enable certain views about the nature of God to be articulated, but the identification of God with a human father is not complete: there are always aspects of human fatherhood which cannot be attributed to God. For example, with the exception of Jesus whose conception is claimed to be asexual, the metaphor is not intended to include the physical conception of children, even though that is a defining quality of human fatherhood. The use of this metaphor is actually a selective attribution to God of some of the features of human fatherhood, but not all of them. Although the metaphor may be helpful to some believers, for many others it is problematic because the behaviour of actual fathers may contradict the positive image of a loving parent that the metaphor is intended to promote. For example, fathers are often absent or emotionally distant from their children, and may be abusive or violent towards them. There are many aspects of human fatherhood that are inappropriate for use in a description of God even, perhaps, as many Christian feminists argue, the metaphor itself.

The juxtaposition of two terms in a metaphor does not amount to an identity between them: 'God' and 'father' are not the same. Metaphorical speech contains within itself its own limit. 'Metaphor always has the character of "is" and "is not": an assertion is made but as a likely account rather than a definition' (McFague, 1987, p. 33). Thus, the metaphorical language of Christian theology always contains a denial as well as an affirmation. Negation is always close behind affirmation in Christian theology, for God cannot be adequately compared with anything at all.

Ultimately, speech breaks down in the contemplation of a God who transcends all human categories, metaphors and images, and who remains irreducibly mysterious. As Janet

Martin Soskice says: 'The great divine and the great poet have this in common: both use metaphor to say that which can be said in no other way but which, once said, can be recognised by many' (Soskice, 1985, p. 153). Speech about God enables us human beings to give sufficient imaginative definition to our religious commitment for us to be able to give direction to that commitment. However, it tells us nothing about what God is like in essence. *Rather than being an expression of absolute truth, religious language is a metaphorical means of giving form to our faith in the unseen God.*

Whenever we speak about God, we use metaphor and, as several writers on metaphor have pointed out, the danger is always that we will end up being used by our metaphors (e.g. Turbayne, 1962). As Miller Mair, a personal construct psychologist, speaking generally explains: 'The danger is in confusing our metaphors, or inventions, with reality itself. If we do this we are likely to tie ourselves down to our new interpretations, our new pretences, just as we were tied down to the old ones.' In order to counter this danger, Mair argues that it is necessary to develop the ability to use 'as if thinking'; in other words, to keep an awareness of 'the "as if" nature of all our concepts' (Mair, 1977, p. 274). To keep the 'as if' nature of religious belief in mind can be very disturbing because we are aware that all our convictions may be erroneous, that we know nothing for certain, and that at any time we may discover our beliefs dissolving. To live with this awareness is likely to feel very insecure. Far from finding a sure ground for confidence in life through our Christian belief, we recognise the provisionality of all our expressions of faith.

However, even though we know that all our conceptions about God are metaphors, open to change and ultimately false, it is possible to commit ourselves to them and act as if they are true. In so doing, we lead our lives on the basis of our belief whilst remaining continuously open to recognising that we may be mistaken, and that our journey in trust into the depths of God has barely begun. Commitment is another way of speaking about faith. Despite the unavoidable inadequacy, provisionality and corrigibility of all our ideas about God, it is necessary, if we are to live a religious life at all, to commit ourselves to those interpretations that convince us most, but always remaining open to new perspectives and the possibility that we may be mistaken. There is an unavoidable risk in doing so: we might prove to be completely wrong. But there is no way we can escape from this uncertainty. All we can do is put our faith in God and trust that he, she or it will respond to our honest attempts to believe, even if we are completely deluded. The problem is that the insecurity of this way of engaging with religious ideas cannot be tolerated by those Christians who are using their beliefs as means of compensating for their own emotional insecurity; it is the opposite of what they are looking for. *Only those who are able to cope with the disturbing psychological effects of doubt and uncertainty are capable of living with an awareness of the provisionality and fragility of their convictions; those who cannot are forced to delude themselves that they possess a certitude which no mortal human being could ever have.*

Uncertainty and the Renewal of Faith

The tendency to avoid tackling perplexing questions, and to resort to an illusion of certainty, seems to me to be widespread in the Christian churches and to be becoming an ever more dominant trend. It is becoming more and more difficult to debate significant issues in the synods and councils of the churches in a genuine attempt to determine the truth. Very often what happens instead is that either power or politics takes over. In denominations with a strong hierarchical form of government, such as the Roman Catholic Church, the ecclesiastical authorities seek to restrain debate and to impose their own conclusions about tendentious matters, using their power to maintain ideological closure. In more democratic churches, such as the Church of England and the Anglican Communion more generally, it seems to be normal for the deliberations of ecclesiastical institutions to aim more at producing a workable compromise between opposing interest groups than at resolving the issues under examination. Their ongoing conflict is contained by theological fudge and political negotiation because neither side is strong enough to defeat or oust the other. This situation may be an inevitable limitation of large ecclesiastical bodies, but it prevents the churches from giving a coherent intellectual presentation of the gospel to the mainly secular society in which they are placed. It also reinforces the tendency of large numbers of Christians to use their membership of a church as a means to resist the need to think.

Confusingly, the Church has, through much of its history, taught both that God is ultimately unknowable, and also that its own teachings are certain because they are based on God's revelation in Christ. It is high time that this contradiction was acknowledged and dispensed with. *We cannot at the same time be ultimately ignorant of God and possess a revelation of him about whose interpretation we can be certain.* We cannot have it both ways. What I propose is that we take our stand on uncertainty and on a return to the ancient theological insight that the forms of the Christian religion cannot contain or adequately express the mystery of God. They give form to our apprehensions of God and enable us to relate to him through them, but they become obstacles to knowledge of God if we take them to be accurate and guaranteed representations of divine truth. In essence, knowledge of God is experiential not conceptual.

Admitting the provisional and uncertain nature of our beliefs about God takes away one of the major foundations of the Christian complex and makes the Gospel of Conditional Love untenable. Without certainty Christians cannot be sure of the conditions under which God will grant his love and acceptance, nor can they be sure that the teaching promoted by their own Christian communities is true to the gospel or not. They are forced to take responsibility for their own beliefs and to use their own minds to struggle with the ambiguities of faith in the confusing contemporary world. Without certainty ideological closure is not possible, because ideological closure is itself a false claim to certainty. If doubt is possible, if there is more than one possible legitimate interpretation of a text or doctrine, ideological closure dissolves. In a similar manner, internalised oppression is undermined by uncertainty because the authority of the oppressive belief system is put in doubt – it might be mistaken. If we Christians attempt to respond in faith and integrity to the God whom we encounter through the forms of belief which we have been inducted into, we will be repeatedly challenged to expand the limited nature of our conceptions of the divine mystery, and to abandon outmoded convictions and spiritual practices. We will be invited by doubt to begin thinking for ourselves, and to question the diktats of the god of group belonging and the ideological commitments of the community of faith.

What I am proposing is that the Church collectively needs to be stripped of its delusions of grandeur and its pretensions to certainty; to rediscover its sinful and vulnerable humanity and taste the depths of its own doubt and evasion of the truth; to give up its identifications with the truth and authority of God and the practice of protecting the institution and its interests against those who demand honesty, accountability and justice; and to abandon its power drive and clericalism and become a community of equals seeking to serve God. The benefit will be that a Church which has relinquished the delusion of certainty, will be able to use the traditional expressions of Christian belief as a starting point for each believer's journey into God, rather than setting them up unconsciously as a defence against going on that journey; and believers who are relieved of the strain of conforming their thinking to the ideological closure of their particular Church, will be able to open and use their minds to explore the mystery of God, whilst recognising that they can never possess more than provisional forms of belief which do not truly represent the essentially unknowable nature of God.

CHAPTER SIX

A Spirituality of Uncertainty

Summary of Conclusions

In this book I have been seeking to show how the Christian religion, especially when it asserts a false certainty, may become the enemy of both genuine faith and the growth to psychological maturity of its adherents. I began by examining the emotional and communal consequences of the traditional Christian belief in the last judgement and heaven and hell, linking the anxiety of many Christians to the implicit message contained within these doctrines that God's love is conditional rather than unconditional, and describing how mainstream Christianity normatively deals with the tension between these two points of view through promoting 'the Gospel of Conditional Love'. Then I explored the various ways in which Christians' fear of rejection by either God or their ecclesiastical communities may lead them to surrender to the god of group belonging or to make the terrible choice in one form or another, thereby seriously inhibiting their ability to live with integrity as true selves, or to engage with the numerous challenges to Christian conviction arising from both science and contemporary scholarship. After that, I described the manner in which churches are frequently assimilated to the ideologies of the societies in which they are placed, and how the Christian religion is often co-opted to provide a divine justification for particular economic and political arrangements. Then I outlined how the emotional needs of individuals are systemically interconnected in the Christian complex with both ideology and the Gospel of Conditional Love, and identified the integration of the Christian shadow as the place to begin the healing of the complex, pointing out some of the most important aspects of the shadows of both individual Christians and ecclesiastical institutions. Finally, I highlighted the identifications of the Bible or the Church with the truth or authority of God as a particular problem, because they support the quest for certainty which is both a denial of genuine Christian faith and an essential feature of the Gospel of Conditional Love and the Christian complex, let alone the conservative forms of the Christian religion to which they give birth.

The evidence which I have presented shows that the form of the Christian gospel which states that God only forgives and accepts into heaven those who have repented and come to believe in Jesus Christ has given birth to innumerable evils. The empirical effects of this religious conviction upon the individuals and communities who adopt it are often very severe. To summarise, my conclusions are:

- that conditional, exclusionary and dualistic forms of Christian belief, including the Gospel of Conditional Love, give rise to repression, neurosis, projection, scapegoating, persecution, war and genocide, all of which are systemically interconnected in the Christian complex;
- that often Christians who accept these versions of Christian teaching injure their own souls because, in order to believe them, they engage in psychological splitting;
- that the institutional and personal hypocrisy and abuse that are often a feature of the churches and their ordained ministers are encouraged and sustained by these convictions and the dynamics associated with them, and that for this

151

reason these faults must not simply be attributed to the individual inadequacies of a minority of sinners;

- and, finally, that only by overcoming its dualistic split will Christianity be able to be reformed in a manner that will do away with these manifold evils.

Because this form of the Christian religion has given birth to so much evil, and because that evil is the direct product of the psychological and social processes that are necessarily, not accidentally, associated with dualistic Christian beliefs, I contend that we can no longer regard those beliefs as revealed by God. Instead, we must acknowledge them to be merely human creations.

The fundamental problem to which we have to find a solution is the split in the Christian psyche associated with this dualism: the division of the individual personality into acceptable and unacceptable portions, and of the human community into insiders and outsiders, good and evil, sacred and profane. At the same time we must eliminate the role that Christianity plays in creating and sustaining this division with all its dire consequences. It should be obvious that this split is the opposite of the transformed existence which the gospel is supposed to inaugurate. In Christian teaching Christ's death is intended to bring about reconciliation not just between God and human beings, but also between all humans and between the different parts of an individual's personality. Ultimately, the Christian promise is that we will enter the kingdom of God. If the doctrines and practices of the Christian Church built upon the foundation of the Bible produce the opposite effect, there must be something radically wrong with the manner in which the Bible is interpreted, or with the biblical text itself, or with both. My conclusion is that they are both corrupted by human sinfulness and by the conditional, exclusionary and legalistic religion which is both product and cause of the dualistic division at the heart of Christianity.

A recognition of the existence and effects of the Gospel of Conditional Love, the Christian complex and the quest for certainty is an important place to initiate the therapy of traditional Christianity; another is the integration of the Christian shadow; and, a third is the breaking down of the identifications of the Bible or the Church with the truth or authority of God, and their replacement with a recognition that all our supposed knowledge of God is in the form of metaphorical, psychologically and culturally conditioned images, stories and ideas through which we give form and direction to our faith in the unseen God. This is not to deny that God may speak to us through the Bible and other Christian teaching in a special way, or that these are 'inspired' by the Holy Spirit and may even be described as 'revelation' in a carefully defined sense. The question we must now address is how the Scriptures and the Church may mediate a genuine relationship with God to us despite the conditioned nature of all our 'knowledge' of God. How may we read the Bible in a manner that is constructive for faith?

The Human Condition and the Knowledge of God

The Bible may fruitfully be regarded as the normative record of the reactions of people with faith to what they took to be the activity of God in the history of Israel and the life and death of Jesus of Nazareth. This is to adopt an 'as if' approach; *we read the Bible as if it shows the reactions of these people to a God who was genuinely present amongst them.* If we do not do at least this much, there is no point in reading the Bible as a religious text at all. When we read the Bible on this basis, it appears to be the account of the responses of largely unconscious, culturally conditioned, frequently neurotic and vulnerable human beings to the disturbing activity of what they took to be God. We recognise that it contains many projections of unconscious material onto God and Jesus of Nazareth and many ideological narratives and teachings, but we also accept that in the midst of these projections and ideologies it witnesses to the God who, we believe, genuinely provoked a response. This is the case even if that response was psychologically defensive, or an assertion of a false identification with the divine. We also recognise that, even though Christians may have been inspired by the Holy Spirit, rather than being objectively accurate depictions of revealed truth, the interpretations of the Bible that have emerged in the Church over the centuries are equally the products of projections and ideologies which may indeed clothe genuine insights into the nature of the divinity, but may equally be mistaken. The same applies to our own conceptions of Christian truth and those of our religious communities.

There is an irreducible paradox at the heart of the Christian claim that God has been revealed in Jesus Christ: God, if he is to reveal anything of himself at all, must do so in the created world; otherwise we can know nothing of him and no revelation has taken place. Thus, a claim that revelation has taken place is an identification of a specific experience with an epiphany of God. It is to 'deify' the particular as a manifestation of the Spirit of God. However, this identification is a human judgement, which we may believe has been inspired by the Holy Spirit, but which can never be demonstrated to have been so on either rational or empirical grounds. It can only be accepted by faith.

The consequences of this insight for Christian belief may be illuminated by considering the example of the incarnation. If we imagine ourselves as those who met Jesus of Nazareth during his earthly lifetime, what would we have seen that would have indicated to us that Jesus was not just an unusual human being, but God incarnate? To the five physical senses he appeared no different from other men. True, the Gospels say that he did some unusual things, such as turning water to wine, walking on water, healing people, and even raising the dead, and he also gave unusual and provocative teaching; but none of these activities communicated to those whom he met anything other than normal sensory information about Jesus. It was not possible for any of them to 'see' his divinity. Indeed, most of them did not even suspect it. If we follow the presentation of Jesus in the Synoptic Gospels (Matthew, Mark and Luke), before his resurrection, those who were not hostile regarded him as a holy man, a prophet or the Messiah, but not as God. Even Peter's confession that Jesus was 'the Son of God' (Mark 8:27–30) did not amount in that cultural context to a recognition of his divinity. Moreover, after the resurrection the Church was slow to arrive at a definitive belief in Jesus' divinity. It was only over the next three centuries that the fully articulated Christian interpretation of Jesus of Nazareth as the incarnate Second Person of the Holy Trinity gradually evolved.

The fact is that *our beliefs about Jesus Christ are the products of the human imagination, which has clothed the historical Jesus with profound meanings that would not have been visible to anyone seeing him in the flesh*. They are interpretations through which we give meaning to our lives. This does not mean that a belief in the incarnation is false or *merely* a product of the imagination. Rather, it is an insight that arose as a result of the normal processes through which we humans make sense of our experience, and which we accept on the basis of faith. We may believe that God was genuinely incarnate in Jesus of Nazareth and, hence, that his life was a true revelation of the divine mystery, but in order to do so we must also claim that God has 'inspired' the whole process of interpretation. In this sense, we may claim that the Bible's or the Church's teachings have been 'revealed', but there is nothing about them that *can be demonstrated* to communicate God's, rather than a merely human, interpretation of experience.

A Method of Reading the Bible

In view of this fact, I suggest that rather than attempting to find some essential authoritative meaning in the Bible, we should read the whole text as a record of the responses of the Jews and the early Christians to their apprehensions of the presence of God in their midst, created in interaction with their own personal psychologies and social settings. And, rather than seeking to defend the Bible as an exclusive and privileged source of religious knowledge, claimed to be 'revelation', against secular insights that appear to destroy this assertion, we should listen to the secular analyses and then ask how we may understand the Bible as also a communication from God to us in the midst of our finite and conditioned experience. In other words, we should look first at our sources of religious information in an ordinary human way, and only when that investigation has been completed ask how, if at all, God may also be thought to be involved in the processes that led to the writing of the Bible, as well as in its present-day interpretation.

To proceed in this manner is, I believe, in accord with the essential nature of theology. *Theology, far from being a source of certainty, is an interpretative discipline which seeks to make sense of human experience on the basis of a belief in God.* As St Anselm said, it is faith seeking understanding – not knowledge. This method prevents us from taking refuge in intellectual timidity or dishonesty, let alone ideological closure or identification, and it also stops us from falling into the Docetic tendency: we take our human reality absolutely seriously as the place where we encounter God. When we seek to discern the activity of God making himself known to us through the ordinary processes of human life, we use our knowledge of those processes as a tool to help us to recognise the presence of God, rather than being frightened of their reductive possibilities. This means that we can express our findings in the language and concepts of contemporary society and enter into a fruitful debate with other believers and also with non-believers. This is the method which I have used in this book. I have analysed the Christian religion in relation to various relevant secular theories, and I am now attempting to speak from the standpoint of a Christian about the human meeting with God in the light of the interpretations of Christian belief and practice that those theories suggest. In doing so, I am drawing on what seem to me to be helpful insights found in the Christian tradition.

We need also to recognise that the Bible displays a dynamic of disclosure of the mystery of the gospel that is uncertain and paradoxical. A struggle between the religion of exclusion and that of inclusion may be discerned within and between the different books of which it is comprised. Sometimes one and sometimes the other seems to be dominant, but they are interwoven in very intricate patterns. For me, this complexity witnesses to the authenticity of the Bible's account of human experience and the ambiguity, misapprehensions and confusion that arise in the human encounter with what we take to be God. These are primarily what the Bible records. Because its accounts are messy they are true to the human condition and reflect it accurately and, as a consequence, they are able to inform us about the human reaction to God as he seeks to reveal himself in our lives.

Just as in the experience of those who met Jesus of Nazareth, the presence of God in the Bible is invisible and can only be perceived by the eyes of faith. Some of those who saw the miracles that Jesus performed had their eyes opened to his true nature as Son of God; others were blind to his significance, seeing only the human being. St John's Gospel is particularly helpful in this respect. It contains a very great deal about sight and blindness, especially an interpretation of Jesus' miracles, not as proofs of his divinity, but as signs which were capable of opening the eyes of faith to see Jesus' true nature. From John's perspective, the strange and remarkable things Jesus did have significance primarily as anomalies that may prompt people to look again at how they regard the world. Hence, they may be the occasion of an opening of the eyes to the presence of God. They do not function as evidence, let alone proof, of the involvement of God in what Jesus did. To see them in that way is to treat Jesus as a miracle worker who has special access to the power of God and is, therefore, able to perform wonders which 'prove' his identity. To regard Jesus like this is to miss the point and the meaning of the signs that he performed. Reading the Bible is one way in which our eyes may be opened to the presence of God in Christ. However, this does not happen automatically; there is a further obstacle to interpreting the Bible, human sinfulness.

Sin, the Law and the Gospel

I have already indicated that sin is an obstacle to the knowledge of God. St Paul said that sin entered the human race through Adam and subsequently gained power over all of his descendants (Romans 5:12–21). He depicted the Law of God as that which revealed the existence of sin, but paradoxically was unable to break its power; rather it seemed to make it worse. In one startling phrase he says: 'The law was added so that the trespass might increase' (Romans 5:20). Furthermore, we cannot escape from sin by our own efforts: everything that we do is tainted by sin (Romans 7:14–24). This state of affairs is what Christian doctrine indicates by saying that human beings are 'fallen'.

The Genesis account of Adam and Eve is a story which provides an explanation for how this came about, and which perplexingly continues to be the basis of the understanding of human nature in Christian theology, even though numerous Christians no longer believe it to be literally true. Paul placed the figure of Adam at the centre of his exposition of the significance of Jesus. His main contention is that just as in Adam the whole human race became subject to sin and death, so in Christ the whole human race is released from the consequences of the Fall and receives the gift of righteousness and life as a result of his death on the cross (Romans 5:12–21; 1 Corinthians 15:21–2).

Paul's theology ultimately gave rise to the doctrine of *original sin*, classically expounded by St Augustine of Hippo, according to which sin is an inherited condition, which we all acquire before we are born or have had the chance to perform any actions, either good or bad. Because we are descended from Adam, Augustine asserted that we were all present in Adam and with him willed to sin and, hence, share in his guilt. Thus, even babies are justly condemned to hell if they are not baptised (Kelly, 1977, pp. 361–6). He was particularly impressed by the way in which human desires overcome our rational wills and appears to have equated what we would now call the instincts, especially sexuality, with the effects of original sin on human nature. Tragically, this equation has encouraged Christians to view human nature as intrinsically corrupt, and has justified both sadistic styles of child-rearing and masochistic forms of spirituality. It has also frequently supported self-hatred and inappropriate self-sacrifice in the faithful, and has reinforced the internal sense of worthlessness of those who have suffered from emotionally inadequate types of upbringing. Consequently, many believers have been all the more dependent upon the external source of affirmation provided by God and the Christian community in order to gain a compensatory sense of value. This has made them vulnerable to the pressures of group conformity, the dictates of the god of group belonging, spiritual abuse and the terrible choice. Because of this there is a direct line running from Paul's presentation of Adam's sin to the creation of the Christian complex.

If Paul's great explication of the mystery of Christ is to continue to be usable in modern theology, it needs to be freed both from the Adamic myth of origins, which is no longer historically plausible, and from the hostile account of human sexuality, and instinct more generally, found in Augustine's teaching. Therefore, I propose that rather than taking original sin as something wrong in human nature, it should be conceived as an existential disorder. In other words, it refers to something that is intrinsically out of true in the way we experience our existence. We are all born to parents who have been born to parents who have, way back over umpteen generations, been born to parents who could not give them a perfect upbringing, who failed fully to meet their need for unconditional love, and imposed upon them forms of socialisation which produced psychological splitting, repression, projection and scapegoating. Furthermore, we are born into societies that justify their existence using ideologies of superiority and its entailments, inferiority and exclusion, and also frequently employ violence and scapegoating in order to sustain social differentiation and political power. It is simply not possible for any of us to grow up without being inducted into the pattern of existence that Paul calls 'sin'. Nor is it possible for us to escape from the conditioning effects of these influences by efforts of will because our wills are directed by our egos, which themselves incorporate the patterns of sin or disorder to which they have been subjected in their upbringing.

As Paul said, 'all have sinned and fall short of the glory of God' (Romans 3:23). It is clear that he was not referring only to sins in the past before a person became a Christian, because he also complained: 'what I do is not the good I want to do; no, the evil I do not want to do – this I keep on doing. Now if I do what I do not want to do, it is no longer I who do it, but it is sin living in me that does it' (Romans 7:19). He discovered that adherence to the Law of God could not save; it did not overcome sin. This insight continues to be valid when 'sin' is conceived to be the tendency to disobey God which results from the existential conditions into which humans are born, rather than as an inborn defect in human nature itself.

The reason why the Law cannot save may be illuminated by the Jungian and psychoanalytic theories which I have already described, especially Eric Neumann's comments on the Old Ethic, that is, the ethic of the Law. The personalities of members of communities governed by the Law are organised around a division between those actions of the individual which are considered to be good and those considered to be sinful. They seek to eliminate those tendencies and characteristics associated with 'evil' from their own personalities either by acts of will (suppression) or by excluding the existence of those traits from awareness (repression). Repression is the internal equivalent of the scapegoat mechanism (the expulsion or destruction of a non-conformist victim), and also the psychological basis for the existence of scapegoating in social groups: without repression, a group's projection of its own evil onto a victim who is blamed for its occurrence would not be possible. The dynamics of repression are fuelled by covenant theology, in which God's favour is explicitly tied to obedience and his punitive violence to disobedience. As a result, God is experienced as a God whose love is conditional and whose wrath is to be feared. Ironically, the person who attempts to obey the Law is caught in a mode of response to God which makes it impossible to achieve that transformed relationship with him which the Law both promises and requires. This situation is all the more ironical since the Torah, the Jewish Law, is presented in the Bible as the God-given means of relationship with him.

The paradox is that obeying the Law brings us to the point of discovering that the Law cannot bring us into an intimate loving relationship with God. This is what I believe Paul discovered when he met Jesus on the Damascus road. His devotion to the Law, which led him to persecute Christians, was revealed to him as a form of opposition to God, and the paradox that the God-given Law failed to overcome sin, and even increased it, became central to his theology. Unfortunately, numerous Christians who have come after him have turned Christianity back into a religion of Law. However, the 'new Law' proposed by such believers has one very important difference from the Torah of Judaism: it was possible in theory, if very hard, to fulfil the requirements of the Torah, but it is utterly impossible to meet the demands of Christian virtue because they include not just actions, but inner attitudes and thoughts as well. This is why any belief (however subtly disguised) that our relationship with Christ is essentially conditional on the fulfilment of his commandments is bound to produce either a sense of failure and its associated fear of rejection in his followers, or else a psychological split. In the latter case, confidence is only maintained by the unconscious adoption of a spirituality of identification with goodness and truth (again, however subtly disguised) and the repression and projection of the negative sides of the personality, with all the dire consequences that result. These are the two common attitudes found amongst Christians to which I referred at the beginning of this book. We can now see why they are so common.

The realisation of my own inadequacy to fulfil Christ's

commandments has been the catalyst which has led me to reject this perversion of Christian belief. The experience of my own failure and inability to keep this 'new Law' has led me to the discovery of a more profound and truly liberating relationship with Christ. This is the perspective from which I have sought to interpret Paul and the Christian gospel and which, for me, makes practical and psychologically coherent sense of the paradoxes of Paul's theology. The good news is that when we acknowledge that we cannot obey this Law, when our egos are defeated and recognise their incapacity to keep the Law, it becomes possible for us to rediscover the message of grace and freedom which is at the core of the genuine Christian gospel.

However, rejecting the religion of Law brings one into conflict with those who still adhere to it (even though they pretend that it is really Christianity). Because the Law describes itself as God-given those who follow it almost always regard it as unchangeable. From their point of view, what God requires is obedience to his already delivered revelation and commands. Hence, any abandonment or revision of the restrictions demanded by the Law seems to be a surrender to sin and an invitation to practise the evil against which the Law is the God-given defence. And, since it is God-given, any criticism of the Law can only appear to be a form of rebellion against God – blasphemy – but, as Paul eloquently argued, the gospel destroys the distinctions set up by the Law and the sanctions it employs to defend them. Hence, those who adhere to the Law can only regard the gospel as opposed to the will of God. This is why the religious leaders of the Jews had no option but to destroy Jesus, who attacked their interpretation of the Law, and why they were able to regard themselves as right and righteous in so doing, and why modern-day Christian Pharisees attack those who reject their distortion of the Christian tradition.

The Dialectic of the Kingdom of God

Bearing in mind the complexity of the relationship between sin, the Law and the gospel, we are now in a position to understand something of how the redeeming life of God is communicated to us through Jesus of Nazareth. St Mark's Gospel introduces Jesus using these words: 'After John was put in prison, Jesus went into Galilee, proclaiming the good news of God. "The time has come," he said. "The kingdom of God is near. Repent and believe the good news!"' (Mark 1:14). Modern biblical scholars regard the primary message of Jesus' teaching to have been the announcement of the coming of the kingdom. *The kingdom of God* is an ideal state in which everything and everyone live in harmony under the rule of God. It symbolises a transformed form of existence in which human beings are so at one with God and each other that they naturally, without internal or external conflict, behave towards each other in ways that display the fruits of the Spirit (Galatians 5:22); all violence is ended in a realm of peace without conflict because God has changed humans' hearts and they all obey him.

The kingdom is foreseen by many of the Hebrew prophets, for example, Ezekiel: 'I will give them an undivided heart and put a new spirit in them; I will remove from them their heart of stone and give them a heart of flesh. Then they will follow my decrees and be careful to keep my laws' (Ezekiel 11:19–20). Isaiah predicts not just human, but natural harmony:

> The wolf will live with the lamb, the leopard will lie down with the goat, the calf and the lion and the yearling together; and a little child will lead them. The cow will feed with the bear, their young will lie down together, and the lion will eat straw like the ox. The infant will play near the hole of the cobra, and the young child put his hand into the viper's nest. They will neither harm nor destroy on all my holy mountain, for the earth will be

163

full of the knowledge of the LORD as the waters cover the sea. (Isaiah 11:6–9)

The kingdom refers to an eschatological age – the 'eschaton' is the end of time – and symbolises the Christian hope that at the end of time God will finally defeat evil and make the world anew, and, as in Isaiah's vision, the fundamental relationships in this current age, including those between carnivore and hunted, will be transformed.

However, because of its eschatological context, the kingdom of God is a highly elusive concept to apply to this current world. The problem is that there is a relationship of disjunction, rather than one of development or reform, between the kingdom and the existing order. Furthermore, it is God alone who is able to initiate the kingdom. Humans may respond to his activity, but they do not have the power themselves to inaugurate it. Nevertheless, many theologians have recruited the idea of the kingdom of God to support radical political movements seeking to bring about greater social justice. Like other theological images, it is easily co-opted to provide an ideological support for particular political programmes in the current world. However, these thinkers are not without some justification: as well as being of the future beyond history, the kingdom of God is also a present reality. As the theologian Donal Dorr says, 'Jesus presents himself and his Kingdom as the future already realised' (Dorr, 1984, p. 100), and he points out the signs of its presence to his listeners (e.g. Luke 4:18–21).

The question of the connection between the kingdom and this world is a major theme of both modern theology and New Testament criticism. The debates about it are far too extensive to summarise here. However, following the theologians Jürgen Moltmann (1977) and Wolfhart Pannenberg (1969), I accept that there is a dialectical relationship between them. In my understanding, the arrival of the kingdom (antithesis) requires humans to change their present way of life (thesis) in response to its challenge and judgement. Either they do, in which case something of what the kingdom symbolises is incorporated into social and individual life (synthesis), or they resist it, in which case those who promote the kingdom are rejected or persecuted and personal development is inhibited (reversion to the original thesis). If any transformation does occur, however slight, the new state of affairs becomes the situation (new thesis) which the kingdom (new antithesis) then challenges. This dialectical development continues until the eschaton. The kingdom never fully arrives in the world as we know it, but is always the present-and-future rule of God. It may be compared to the idea of infinity: if we start counting we get closer to it, but it is impossible ever to reach it.

In the Bible, especially in its witness to Jesus, this dialectic is displayed in all its subtlety. The main theme of the Synoptic Gospels (Matthew, Mark and Luke) is precisely the in-breaking of the kingdom in the person of Jesus of Nazareth and the manner in which he was received. They describe the dialectic of the kingdom as it was played out in the interaction between Jesus, the disciples, the leaders of the Jews and the ordinary people. St John's Gospel gives a brilliant exposition of this dialectic in its account of the struggle between light and darkness and of the paradoxes of true sight and blindness, and St Paul provides a most astute and suggestive account of its dynamics in the relations between sin, the Law and the gospel.

The Church and the Dialectic of the Kingdom of God

The dialectic of the kingdom of God is the essential key to developing a form of the Christian religion that is free from psychological splitting, and is expressed through Christian institutions that do not identify themselves with the truth and authority of God. The kingdom is a symbol for the eschatological rule of God which is both a present and a future reality, constantly entering the contingent world and yet remaining outside it. We experience its presence as at the same time judgement and forgiveness, and this enables us to repent and incorporate something of its meaning into our lives now.

However, because we exist in an imperfect environment and we are ourselves psychologically incomplete, we are likely very rapidly to assimilate what we have grasped into the structures of finitude and sin. In particular, we are liable to identify what we think we have perceived of God with the divine mystery itself and mentally to separate our own formulations from, and treat them as superior to, ordinary contingent knowledge, as the Church has frequently done to the Bible, doctrine, and itself. Consequently, the kingdom comes to us next as a judgement upon our new identifications. This progression is how the dialectic of the kingdom is experienced in our everyday existence. If we engage with it consciously, it can provide the basis for a very rich spirituality capable of handling the paradoxes of God's presence in the human condition without resorting to splitting.

From this point of view it should be clear that there is much in common between the Synoptic Gospels' accounts of the Pharisees and the Christian Church today. The Church is a congeries of human institutions which attempts to witness to the kingdom of God. It is subject to all the sinfulness and contingency of the fallen world, including the tendency to identify itself, at least in essence, with the goodness and truth of God – the Christian version of the Pharisees' mistake. Indeed, it very often replicates the religion of the Law.

In relation to the dialectic of the kingdom of God, despite its own ambiguous connection to the kingdom, the role of the Church is to prepare us for its coming. On the positive side, the Church does this by witnessing to the life, death and teaching of Christ and providing forms of worship and Christian fellowship which encourage and sustain the devout as they seek to respond to the invitation of Christ to enter into a relationship with him. However, on the negative side, the Church is often so compromised by identification with the truth and authority of God, abusive and power-driven structures or officials, ideological assimilation, ideological closure and sinful behaviour in general that both churchgoers and those who do not attend are made aware of a huge gap between its claims and its reality.

If taken seriously, the affirmations which the Church makes about itself lead to a point of contradiction, a crisis of faith. This has certainly been my experience. Given both the historical and the contemporary record of the Church, to experience it as a witness to God's grace in a troubled and fallen world is to experience contradiction. I find it hard to believe that anyone who is free enough of psychological defences to allow him- or herself to look at what actually happens in the Church, can do so without being severely disturbed to the point of wondering where God is in the institution. It is not surprising that people become disillusioned and leave the Church or give up their Christian faith. What is surprising is that anyone stays inside and takes the Church's claims seriously!

However, this crisis is not a negative thing in itself, however bad it may feel. Given the way human beings function, we should not be surprised that the Church is as it is. It is, after all, we who are its members. When we experience the absurdity of the Church's teachings about itself, we may also discover the absurdity of our own pretensions to live Christian lives – we too exist within the dialectic of the kingdom. This discovery may lead to an experience of brokenness which destroys any identification we have made with the good. We may experience the hollowness and futility of our own religion and the truth that we are sinners. Paradoxically, as Sebastian Moore indicates, this is the point at which the Christian religion may be discovered to be a source of grace, and God to be the one who loves us just as we are. We discover that we have rejected and crucified Christ and, in acknowledging our opposition to God, we encounter at the same time his great love, which refuses to reject us. We enter into the combined experience of judgement and mercy which the coming of the kingdom brings, and we are enabled to repent.

From this perspective, recognising the location of the Church in the dialectic of the kingdom is a very useful exercise. We can take its claims seriously whilst acknowledging that they make no rational sense outside of the perspective provided by the dialectic itself. Such an attitude may protect us from the complete lunacy of trying to defend a belief that what the Church says about itself is true through resorting to mentally splitting off and denying all those aspects of its behaviour and teaching that contradict that belief. Between the alternatives of disillusion and defensive blindness, neither of which is fruitful for the life of faith, there is the third possibility of recognising the workings of the dialectic of the kingdom in the Church. This is a route to an experiential discovery of the truth of *the Church's fundamental identity as a witness to Christ within the dialectic of the kingdom.*

Theological Disputes and the Dialectic of the Kingdom of God

The Christian religion and the Church are means of giving form to our apprehensions of God which have the capacity to bring us to a genuine encounter with God. If we permit ourselves to move out of the constraints of our previous convictions and to risk opening ourselves to the disturbing activity of the Spirit of God, we may experience a genuine development in our spiritual lives and a genuine growth towards holiness. Such openness may be further facilitated by a recognition of the position of theological thinking in the dialectic of the kingdom. I have described the ancient distinction between apophatic and cataphatic theology. It seems to me that this mirrors the division between the kingdom of God and the current world order. Apophatic theology is based on an apprehension of the hiddenness of the divine mystery which we cannot know, whatever intimations of it we may believe we have perceived. Cataphatic theology proclaims those things which we believe we know about God. In terms of the dialectic, apophatic theology stands in the place of the kingdom, and cataphatic in the place of the Law. Cataphatic gives form to what we have experienced, but is always under the judgement of apophatic, which holds firm to the one truth that we do know, namely, that God can only be known by unknowing.

This is why the language and the images we use to describe God must be subject to a constant critique. Throughout this book I have referred to God using the male gender. This is because it seemed to me that to do so would better convey the problems associated with the representations of God in traditional Christianity, especially those connected to the abuse of power. In contrast, changing the language we use to depict God may be of great assistance to Christians who are attempting to avoid an identification of their cataphatic theological formulations with the reality of God; adopting a different gender for God or unusual imagery may startle believers into a renewed apprehension of her impact on their lives, as feminist theologians have demonstrated.

In contrast, there is always the danger that we will foreclose our engagement with the Spirit by retreating to prepared positions and assimilating what we have newly experienced of God to them, thereby creating a new Law. Regrettably, this is what those in the Church who assert a false certainty do; they resist that insecurity and doubt which is a necessary part of spiritual growth. The irony is that if they embraced uncertainty they would be aligning themselves not only with the sanctifying work of the Holy Spirit, but also with the scepticism of the postmodern society in which they are situated. Of course, postmodern suspicion is not the same as theological unknowing, but there is, I am convinced, sufficient in common to provide the meeting point for a creative debate between Christianity and contemporary thought.

A further irony is that the Church is being forced to face the corrosive effects of contemporary challenges to its traditional beliefs whether it wishes to or not. Falling numbers of worshippers, recent scandals and the cumulative impact of secular scientific and intellectual enquiry over many centuries have combined to make the Church less and less credible to the general population. At some point, one would have thought, such decline must surely compel the Church to genuine self-reflection and an abandonment of its delusions about itself. However, rather than developing a co-operative attempt to discover what is going wrong, most denominations have fallen into sterile internal bickering between their liberal and conservative wings in which both sides blame the other for the decline in churchgoing. Whilst these disputes continue in the mutually dismissive form which they generally take, the Christian Church will simply experience the corrosive effects of frustration, resentment, anger and bitterness rather than the healing disillusionment brought by a genuine encounter with the Spirit of God.

The dialectic of the kingdom provides a standpoint which may enable these disputants to understand better how their different perspectives complement each other. If all parties in the current theological disputes were to recognise the dialectic of the kingdom as the context in which they debate, they might gain a more modest and more tentative perspective on the truth of their own tenets, and be inspired to enter into a co-operative engagement with those with whom they disagree in an attempt to listen together to the judgement of God on the present state of the Church. As far as I can see, all parties in the current ecclesiastical battles are genuine in their convictions – if they were not, they would hardly bother to fight. All are seeking either to defend or to advance interpretations of the gospel which they are convinced represent the will of God, and all acknowledge their *personal* fallibility or sinfulness – however much they may defend the certainty or holiness of a particular source of religious authority.

In terms of the dialectic of the kingdom, the conservatives represent the phase when there is an established integration of the gospel message into the life of the Church – in other words, the phase of Law – one which is ripe for a new encounter with the kingdom in the phase of judgement and reformation. In this respect, the conservatives are the Pharisees of the contemporary Church. However, this comment should not be taken as denigrating them. We have to remember that the Pharisees are the best that the Law can produce, and that for most of the time the Church exists in this world as an institution of the Law, even though, paradoxically, the Law that it practises is the gospel. The conservatives are the ones who maintain and police the tradition whilst also attempting in all sincerity to obey the commandments of God as they understand them, often at great personal cost.

From this perspective it would be easy to see the liberals as representing the coming of the kingdom as a judgement on the conservative position. And many on the liberal side, whether consciously or unconsciously, appear to identify themselves as latter-day apostles proclaiming the gospel to a group of latter-day Pharisees, who do not have ears to hear the good news. *However, this is a serious and arrogant mistake.* Even though the liberals represent the voice of change, this does not necessarily mean that they also represent the voice of Christ or that what they propose has anything whatsoever to do with the intentions of God. This point is essential. *Liberal reforms may just as easily be the product of sin or error as of the Holy Spirit*, whatever theological justifications may be advanced on their behalf. Liberals, just as much as conservatives, often appear to have fallen into an identification of their positions with the will of God. In this respect, they too are Pharisees, even if their Pharisaism is more disguised than that of the conservatives.

The essential point is that neither the liberals nor the conservatives may legitimately identify their beliefs with God's truth, because neither the liberals nor their conservative opponents are in a position *unequivocally* to know what God wants. All that both sides can do is act out of their *own convictions* in the belief that God is faithful and will correct their errors. Whenever anyone asserts that she or he has definitive or certain knowledge of the will of God on the grounds of 'biblical truth' or 'the teaching of the universal Church' or 'the presence of God amongst the poor' or whatever, she or he crosses the boundaries of the limitations set upon the human ability to speak about the mystery which we call God. Unfortunately, such claims are all too common at the moment and *they are deadly to authentic Christian faith.*

It would assist us all to avoid such destructive claims if, rather than using it as a source of proof texts for our convictions, we always read the Bible as if we are priests, scribes and Pharisees who have taken over the Word of God for our own purposes, and resist the words of Jesus which challenge that strategy. It would further this process if we all adopted the habit of assuming that our interpretations of the Bible may be erroneous and that our own Christian commitment may be a form of Pharisaism and, therefore, a disguised rebellion against God. Instead of identifying our present religious position with that of God, we need to act on the presumption that we are likely to be defending a form of belief which supports a legalistic kind of religion or a particular ideological stance and is, therefore, in need of reform. When we read the Gospels we must listen to the words of Jesus as criticisms of ourselves, and ask ourselves to what extent they may apply to our present religious practices. *How far have we turned the words of humans into the words of God?*

If we read the Bible as if we are the Pharisees who have come to rely upon our conception of what God wills to justify our existence to God and to earn his favour, then we will be better able to hear the teaching of the gospel as something that destroys the illusion that we can meet any conditions that God may lay down for his acceptance. When we have got so far, we may also find it possible to hear the gospel's witness to the coming of Christ as the one who overturns the whole religion of conditional love. However, we can only do this, if we are willing to face the fact that much of our religion is a form of rebellion against God. We have to live with the paradox that the Church's role in the economy of salvation is to witness to the one who judges the Church, and that any genuine attempt to follow Christ will in all probability lead into conflict with the Church and provoke its rejection.

The Limits to Jesus' Knowledge

Before concluding we need to pause to consider a facet of the New Testament's presentation of Jesus which is potentially fatal to the argument of this book. The picture of Jesus in the Gospels is a very uncomfortable one, which is what one would expect; if he truly represents the coming of the kingdom of God, his words and actions are going to be very disturbing. Certainly, that is how the Jewish leaders of his time experienced them and we should not expect to be any different, since we too belong to religious communities dominated by Law. Even so, there is a particular difficulty in some of the content of what Jesus is recorded to have said: he expresses a belief in a final judgement (e.g. Matthew 10:28; Luke 16:24–6; Luke 17:1b-2). It may well be that Jesus himself believed in the final division of humankind.

If my thesis that God is unconditionally loving and there is no final division of humanity into the saved and the damned is correct, some explanation for these sayings must be found. If none can be, we must concede that Christianity is indeed essentially and irredeemably dualistic, and that the terrible evils arising from the Christian complex which have dogged its history are simply a necessary consequence of fundamental Christian beliefs when they interact with the damaged psyches and societies of fallen human beings. There would be no option but to conclude that billions of people over the centuries have been deceived into believing in a religion which promises peace, but which, because of this dualism, will always and necessarily produce division and conflict in human relations.

My reply is to look at Jesus himself in the context of the dialectic of the kingdom of God, and to use this perspective as a basis for a Christology which is consistent with my reasoning. The doctrine of the incarnation is helpful in this respect. It states that Jesus was both God and human; in him there was a complete union of a human life and God's being. This idea is a mystery beyond human comprehension and, as a result, it has given rise to some pretty strange ideas about Jesus at the popular level. Christians often seem to treat Jesus as a split personality and may refer to what he experienced 'as God' in contrast to what he experienced 'as a human being'. For instance, I have heard someone say in a Bible study group that Jesus was ignorant as a human, but all-knowing because he was God.

The identification of Jesus' *human* consciousness with *God's* own awareness seems to have slipped into Christian thinking under the cover of the doctrine of the incarnation, and then to have been used to support more general identifications of the Bible and the Church with the knowledge or goodness of God. If we are to break these identifications it will also be necessary to break that of Jesus' humanity with God's omniscience. One way of doing this is to recognise that Jesus the human existed within the dialectic of the kingdom as much as any other person, and to seek to discern the dialectic of the kingdom at work in the historical teaching of Jesus in the same way as we look for it in the Bible as a whole.

In all essentials Jesus' human nature was the same as ours; the only difference was that he was united with the hidden reality of God in a manner of which we cannot conceive. Obviously, this means that he expressed the life of God in human terms in a totally unique way, but it does not also mean that his human consciousness was able to conceptualise the mystery of God in terms that were free from the contingency of human culture and language and their ultimate inability to image God. We need to get away from any idea that Jesus' divinity somehow gave him privileged access as a member of the human race to God's knowledge. As a human being he shared in human limitation including mortality, ignorance and error. He appears to have believed in the cosmology of his time and to have regarded the Hebrew Scriptures as literally true, neither of which beliefs are any longer justified. Furthermore, scholars have shown that much of his teaching is a product of his Jewish environment. Inevitably, he used concepts and images drawn from the world of thought into which he was born, and these included the Jewish religion of covenant and Law with its entailments, exclusion and condemnation. Many passages in the Hebrew Bible suggest that the kingdom of God will be inaugurated by a time of radical social and physical disruption, often called 'the Day of the Lord', when God will terrorise humanity, especially those who are in rebellion against him, and at the end of which humankind will be brought to judgement. What is remarkable is the degree to which Jesus confronted and reconfigured the religion he inherited but, even so, we should not expect his original words, even when we can discern which they were, to be either free from cultural conditioning or without error. Rather, what we should anticipate is to witness the kingdom of God breaking into our world through them and provoking a response of repentance or resistance.

If we interpret Jesus' teaching as a product of the presence of the transformative power of God (which is what the kingdom of God is in essence) in the life of this finite human being, we can observe its effects upon both himself and others, even though we cannot describe the mode of God's presence in him. However, the full implications of the coming of the kingdom into his religious world are unlikely to have been clear to Jesus himself. Even if he was God and was sinless, the transformation of the conceptual world into which he was born by the kingdom of God had not yet taken place – indeed, it still has not been completed. The teachings of Jesus were culturally conditioned and limited by the finite, socially constructed human landscape and religious context in which they developed. Rather than being the final and definitive revelation from God, they may be regarded as the first stage in a process, which Jesus inaugurated, of the incarnation of the kingdom of God in human culture which continues to be guided by the Holy Spirit.

In the life of Jesus as a whole, and the behaviour of those whom he met, we may perceive a revelation of what happens when God enters our lives: we betray or kill him, but God refuses to reject us and he refuses to stay dead and rises again. This truth is symbolised by the resurrection, which reveals the power of God to overcome human evil at its greatest not by force, but by love. The life of God cannot be destroyed and, however often we 'murder' Christ's Spirit within us, he always returns promising us new life and somehow mysteriously as we wrestle with God, discovering in the process the truth of who we are, both good and evil, we may be transformed.

A Spirituality of Uncertainty and the Reform of the Church

Despite all that I have said, I must stress how often Christianity has inspired its followers to live lives of selfless devotion to others. However much they may have been compromised by psychological inadequacies or ideological assimilation or Pharisaism, there have been numerous individuals involved in mission, pastoral care, social reform, medical and famine relief, education and other caring activities who have sacrificed a great deal for the sake of others. This book is primarily about the shadow side of Christianity, a fact which must not be allowed to obscure the reality of its light side and the benefits which, in spite of its negative aspects, Christianity has brought to humanity.

Also, I have said little about the positive side of congregational life. There is very often a remarkable degree of active caring for each other within a congregation and of authentic social concern expressed both in fundraising for charity and in direct practical assistance where that is possible. There are many kind, good, humane people in the Christian churches. This includes those who are strongly influenced by the Christian complex who, precisely for this reason, may show considerable consideration for others and much generosity. Fortunately, one of the expectations of church members is that they seek to emulate Christ's involvement with the poor and outcast. Paradoxically, this is the case even in parishes which are very supportive of a politically conservative ideology. The teaching of Christ has the potential to destabilise, at least to some extent, even the most stratified forms of social organisation: Christians have always been required to attend to the needs of others (James 2:14–26; 1 John 3:17–18) if they are to regard themselves as truly Christian; and even if – possibly because – such caring has become part of the New Law, it has produced much good.

These are the positive consequences of Christian belief, which paradoxically exist alongside a shadow side which is often very dark indeed. In this book I have been tracing the systemic connection between the light and the dark sides of the Christian religion. What I have been arguing is that, despite the existence of the Christian shadow, the witness of Christianity to a God who loves us unconditionally may be trusted, and a thoroughgoing acceptance of this witness would lead to a radical reform of mainstream Christian belief and practice; and, in addition, that even though so compromised and so often corrupt, the Christian religion plays a positive role in God's purposes. Since at the human level it is the product of human psychology and cultural conditioning, Christianity is inevitably assimilated to the human tendency to identify ourselves and our communities with the favour of God by differentiating ourselves from others whom we denigrate or reject. In other words, the Christian religion as it currently exists is for the most part a product of Law and sin, replicating precisely the pattern of religion that, I believe, Jesus came to reveal and to transcend. He did this on the cross, but even so the cross is not a static victory achieved once and for all and whose benefits may be installed as the prized possessions of a fixed institution called 'the Church'. Rather, the cross is the inauguration of a dynamic dialectical form of relationship with God, into which we are invited to enter precisely by rejecting the exclusionary tendencies of formal religion.

The essential insight which I have tried to communicate in this book is that the Christian religion will only be able to heal its divided soul, and the many ills which originate from it, if ecclesiastical bodies and individual Christians are prepared to abandon the Gospel of Conditional Love, face their own shadows and give up any claim to certain knowledge about God. The time has come when the Church must choose between, on the one hand, certainty and conditional love and, on the other hand, uncertainty and unconditional love. The division in the heart of Christianity can only be healed if it chooses uncertainty and unconditional love and recognises that rather than already possessing the truth about God, it exists in the dialectic of the kingdom of God and is constantly subject to both sin and the liberating activity of the Holy Spirit. However, the Church as a whole is unlikely to make this choice. In the meantime, we ordinary Christians should do what we can, seeking to influence our denominations to change and endeavouring, as far as possible, to respond to the message of the good news in our own lives, knowing that, in so far as we succeed, we are likely to come into conflict with both the Church and the world.

I have not attempted to suggest how the structures of the institutional churches may be reformed in the light of the dialectic of the kingdom. Different denominations have many different forms of organisation; some have deacons, priests and bishops, others ministers, and others no ordained ministry at all. It seems as if every conceivable type of church order has been tried, but since all are subject to the same constraints of the human condition, they all tend to become new expressions of the Law. This is precisely what my exposition of the dialectic of the kingdom of God predicts. There is no escape from the limitations, disorderliness and sinfulness of this world, and the potential it contains for the gospel to be assimilated to and identified with particular religious communities.

I do not believe that any reform could ever take place as the result of which the Church would consistently live as if it were already in the kingdom of God. In contrast, the kind of reform I am proposing is precisely that, rather than being ignored or denied, this impossibility and our ultimate ignorance of God needs to be made the conscious and deliberate foundation of all the contingent forms in which we seek to express and live out our Christian faith. If this were to happen, many obstacles to the activity of the Holy Spirit would be removed. Even so, I do not imagine that the time will ever come when the Church will be free from rigidity, authoritarianism and intellectual closure; these are too much a part of ordinary human psychology and social structures and too much the product of sin to disappear.

Christianity does not redeem us out of the human condition. Rather, it witnesses to the presence of God within that condition at its worst, and to his power to lead us into a profound relationship of love despite that condition's most destructive effects. The paradox is that when we take Christianity's claims seriously, attempt to respond to them within the Church and discover both our inability to follow Christ and the corruption of ecclesiastical institutions, we may also be released into an experience of God that transcends the Church. *We may have a genuine and transformative encounter with Christ as we participate in the dialectic of the kingdom through our membership of the Church.*

Even now, the good news is that if we take it seriously, our commitment to the Christian religion will lead us to a point of disillusionment and judgement in which our religion, both institutional and individual, is revealed as hopelessly compromised and in many respects a product of our sinfulness. At that point, we may be freed from a dependence upon ecclesiastical structures and discover the God of unconditional love to whom Christ witnesses. We may enter an experience of grace, mercy and love which reveals the Christian religion and the institutional Church, despite their corruption, to have been all along a route to God.

REFERENCES

Abbott, W.M. (ed.) (1966). *The Documents of Vatican II*. London: Geoffrey Chapman

Alison, J. (2001). *Faith beyond Resentment: Fragments Catholic and Gay*. London: Darton, Longman & Todd

Aquinas, T. (1964). *Summa Theologiae*, ed. H. McCabe. London: Eyre & Spottiswoode

Bateson, G. (1972). *Steps to an Ecology of Mind: Mind and Nature*. New York: Ballantine Books

Brown, A. (1990). Vatican Denies Right of Dissent to Theologians. *Independent*, 27 June, 10

Brown, P. (1969). *Augustine of Hippo: A Biography*. London: Faber and Faber

Byrne, L. (2000). *The Journey is My Home*. London: Hodder & Stoughton

Church of England (1985). *Faith in the City: The Report of the Archbishop of Canterbury's Commission on Urban Priority Areas*. London: Church House Publishing

  (1991). *Issues in Human Sexuality: A Statement by the House of Bishops*. London: Church House Publishing

Church Society (undated). *Aids and the Judgment of God*. London: Church Society

Clark, J. (2001). Americans are Blind to Barbarians at their Gates. *The Times*, 15 September 2001, 18

Dallos, R. & Draper, R. (2000). *An Introduction to Family Therapy: Systemic Theory and Practice*. Buckingham and Philadelphia: Open University Press

Donohoe, M. (2002). Not all the Religious were Bad. *Irish Times*, 1 November, 18

Dorr, D. (1984). *Spirituality and Justice*. Dublin: Gill and MacMillan

Dowling, J. (2002) Letter to the Editor, *Sunday Independent*, 20 October

Fiddes, P. (2000). *Participating in God: A Pastoral Doctrine of the Trinity*. London: Darton, Longman & Todd

Fortunato, J.E. (1987). *Aids: The Spiritual Dilemma*. San Francisco: Harper & Row

Freeman, D. (1991). *Victim Power: The Clinical and Philosophical Paradox of Nazi and Jew*. London: Guild of Pastoral Psychology Lecture No. 238

Freud, S. (1901/1960). The Psychopathology of Everyday Life. In J. Strachey (ed. and tr.), *The Standard Edition of the Complete Psychological Works of Sigmund Freud Vol. 5.* London: Hogarth

Gutierrez, G. (1999). The Task and Content of Liberation Theology. In C. Rowland (ed.), *The Cambridge Companion to Liberation Theology* (pp. 19–38). Cambridge: Cambridge University Press

Guggenbühl-Craig, A. (1971). *Power in the Helping Professions.* Dallas, Texas: Spring

Higton, T. (undated). *Letter to the Clergy of the Church of England*

Hull, J. (1991) *What Prevents Christian Adults from Learning?* Philadelphia: Trinity Press International

Jacobi, J. (1973). *The Psychology of C.G. Jung: An Introduction with Illustrations.* New Haven and London: Yale University Press

Jacobi, M. (1999). *Jungian Psychotherapy and Contemporary Infant Research.* London and New York: Routledge

Johnson, D. & Von Vonderon, J. (1991). *Subtle Power of Spiritual Abuse: Recognising and Escaping Spiritual Manipulation and False Spiritual Authority.* Minneapolis: Bethany House

Jung, C.G. (1923/1971). Definitions. In C.G. Jung, *Psychological Types. The Collected Works Vol. 6,* tr. H.G. Baynes, rev. R.F.C. Hull (pp. 408–86). London: Routledge

(1928/1966a). The Therapeutic Value of Abreaction. In C.G. Jung, *The Practice of Psychotherapy. The Collected Works Vol. 16,* tr. H.G. Baynes, rev. R.F.C. Hull, 2nd edn (pp. 129–38). London: Routledge

(1928/1966b). The Relations between the Ego and the Unconscious. In C.G. Jung, *Two Essays on Analytical Psychology. The Collected Works Vol. 7,* tr. H.G. Baynes, rev. R.F.C. Hull, 2nd edn (pp. 123–304). London: Routledge

(1935/1977). The Tavistock Lectures. In C.G. Jung, *The Symbolic Life: Miscellaneous Writings. The Collected Works Vol. 18,* tr. H.G. Baynes, rev. R.F.C. Hull (pp. 5–182). London and New York: Routledge and Kegan Paul

(1936/1937/1968). The Concept of the Collective Unconscious. In C.G. Jung, *The Archetypes and the Collective Unconscious. The Collected Works Vol. 9, Part 1,* tr. H.G. Baynes, rev. R.F.C. Hull, 2nd edn (pp. 42–53). London: Routledge

(1937/1969). Psychological Factors Determining Human Behaviour. In C.G. Jung, *The Structure and Dynamics of the Psyche. The Collected Works Vol. 8,* tr. H.G. Baynes, rev. R.F.C. Hull, 2nd edn (pp. 114–25). London: Routledge

(1938/1969). Psychology and Religion. In C.G. Jung, *Psychology and Religion: West and East. The Collected Works Vol. 11,* tr. H.G. Baynes, rev. R.F.C. Hull, 2nd edn (pp. 3–105). London: Routledge

(1939/1968). Conscious, Unconscious, and Individuation. In C.G. Jung, *The Archetypes and the Collective Unconscious. The Collected Works Vol. 9,*

Part 1, tr. H.G. Baynes, rev. R.F.C. Hull, 2nd edn (pp. 275–89). London: Routledge

(1948/1969). A Review of the Complex Theory. In C.G. Jung, *The Structure and Dynamics of the Psyche. The Collected Works Vol. 8*, tr. H.G. Baynes, rev. R.F.C. Hull, 2nd edn (pp. 92–104). London: Routledge

(1951/1968). *Aion: Researches into the Phenomenology of the Self. The Collected Works Vol. 9, Part 2*, tr. H.G. Baynes, rev. R.F.C. Hull, 2nd edn. London: Routledge

(1956/1977). On the Discourses of the Buddha. In C.G. Jung, *The Symbolic Life: Miscellaneous Writings. The Collected Works Vol. 18*, tr. H.G. Baynes, rev. R.F.C. Hull (pp. 697–9). London and New York: Routledge and Kegan Paul

(1957/1970). The Undiscovered Self. In C.G. Jung, *Civilisation in Transition. The Collected Works Vol. 10*, tr. H.G. Baynes, rev. R.F.C. Hull, 2nd edn (pp. 245–305). London: Routledge

(1968). *The Archetypes and the Collective Unconscious. The Collected Works Vol. 9, Part 1*, tr. H.G. Baynes, rev. R.F.C. Hull, 2nd edn. London: Routledge

(1973). *Experimental Researches. The Collected Works Vol. 2*, tr. H.G. Baynes, rev. R.F.C. Hull. London: Routledge

Kalsched, D.E. (2003). Response to James Astor. *Journal of Analytical Psychology*, 48: 201–5

Kelly, J.N.D. (1977). *Early Christian Doctrines*, 5th edn. London: Adam and Charles Black

Kelly, K.T. (1993). 'Do We Believe in a Church of Sinners?' *The Way*, Vol. 33, No. 2, 106–16

Klein, M. (1959/1988). Our Adult World and its Roots in Infancy. In M. Klein. *Envy and Gratitude and Other Works 1946–1963* (pp. 247–63). London: Virago

Liechty, J. (1995). Christianity and Identity in Ireland: A Historical Perspective. Lecture given at Christianity, Culture and Identity Conference, ECONI, 4 November

Longley, C. (2002). *Chosen People: The Big Idea that Shapes England and America*. London: Hodder & Stoughton

Lossky, V. (1957). *The Mystical Theology of the Eastern Church*. Cambridge & London: James Clarke

McAleese, M. (1997). *Reconciled Being, Love in Chaos: The John Main Seminar 1997*. London and Berkhamsted: Medio Media/Arthur James

McFague, S. (1987). *Models of God: Theology for an Ecological, Nuclear Age*. London: SCM Press

McGarry, P. (2001). Two Tribes. *Irish Times Weekend Review*, 7 July, 1

McGlinchey, P. (1996). The Threefold Cord: The Fusion of Patriotism, Violence and the Gospel in Ireland. *Frontiers: Evangelical Perspectives on Faith and Society*, Autumn 1996, 36–42

Main, J. (1985). *The Way of Unknowing*. London: Darton, Longman & Todd

Mair, M. (1977). Metaphors for Living. In A.L. Landfield (ed.), *Nebraska Symposium on Motivation 1976* (pp. 243–90). Nebraska: University of Nebraska Press

Miller, A. (1983). *For Your Own Good: The Roots of Violence in Childrearing*. London: Virago

(1985). *Thou Shalt Not Be Aware: Society's Betrayal of the Child*. London: Pluto Press

(1987). *The Drama of Being a Child and the Search for the True Self*. London: Virago

Minear, P.S. (1984). *Matthew: The Teacher's Gospel*. London: Darton, Longman & Todd

Moltmann, J. (1977). *The Church in the Power of the Spirit*. San Francisco: Harper

Moore, S. (1977). *The Crucified is No Stranger*. London: Darton, Longman & Todd

Moorman, J.R.H. (1963). *A History of the Church in England*. London: Adam and Charles Black

Moses, R. (1989). Projection, Identification, and Projective Identification: Their Relation to the Political Process. In J. Sandler (ed.), *Projection, Identification, Projective Identification* (pp. 117–50). London: Karnac Books

Neumann, E. (1973). *Depth Psychology and a New Ethic*. San Francisco: Harper Torchbooks

O'Neill, S. (1994). Vicar Casts Out Adulterers from his Flock. *Daily Telegraph*, Tuesday 14 June, 3

Orwell, G. (1954). *Nineteen Eighty-Four*. Harmondsworth, Middlesex: Penguin Books

Pannenberg, W. (1969). *Theology and the Kingdom of God*. Philadelphia: Westminster

Perera, S.B. (ed.) (1986). *The Scapegoat Complex: Towards a Mythology of Shadow and Guilt*. Toronto: Inner City Books

Petterson, Revd. B. (1991). The Pastor's Patch: 6. The Holiday Resort. *Expository Times*, 103, December, 67–71

Reeves, M. (1987) Compassion and Common Sense: Creative Caring in the AIDS Crisis. In *AIDS: A Diocesan Response* (pp. 14–20). Oxford: Oxford Diocesan Board of Social Responsibility

Rowland, C. (1999). Introduction: The Theology of Liberation. In C. Rowland (ed.), *The Cambridge Companion to Liberation Theology* (pp. 1–16). Cambridge: Cambridge University Press

Sharkey, J. (2001). Letter to the Editor. *Irish Times*, 30 March

Sobel, D. (1999). *Galileo's Daughter: A Drama of Science and Faith*. London: Fourth Estate

Solignac, P. (1982). *The Christian Neurosis*. London: SCM Press

Soskice, J.M. (1985). *Metaphor and Religious Language*. Oxford: Clarendon Press

Stein, M. (1998). *Jung's Map of the Soul: An Introduction*. Chicago & La Salle, Illinois: Open Court

Stern, D.N. (1998). *The Interpersonal World of the Infant: A View from Psychoanalysis and Developmental Psychology*. London: Karnac Books

Turbayne, C.M. (1962). *The Myth of Metaphor*. New Haven & London: Yale University Press

Tyrell, C.W. (1988). Letter to the Editor. *Church Times*, 25 November

von Franz, M-L. (1980), *Projection and Re-collection in Jungian Psychology: Reflections of the Soul*. La Salle & London: Open Court

Walker, A. (1989). Letter to the Editor. *Church Times*, 10 March

Ward, W. (1989). Courtesy and the Soft-centred Church. *Church Times*, 28 April, 20

Wehr, D.S. (2000). Spiritual Abuse: When Good People Do Bad Things. In P. Young-Eisendrath & M.E. Miller (eds.), *The Psychology of Mature Spirituality: Integrity, Wisdom, Transcendence* (pp. 47–61). London & Philadelphia: Routledge

Winnicott, D.W. (1960/1965). Ego Distortion in Terms of True and False Self. In D.W. Winnicott, *Maturational Processes and the Facilitating Environment: Studies in the Theory of Emotional Development*, (pp. 140–52). London: Hogarth Press

(1971a). Mirror-role of Mother and Family in Child Development. In D.W. Winnicott, *Playing and Reality* (pp. 130–8). Harmondsworth: Penguin Books

(1986). The Concept of the False Self. In D.W. Winnicott, *Home is Where We Start From* (pp. 65–70). Harmondsworth: Penguin

INDEX

➤✦